CONTENTS

Helion & Company Limited
Unit 8 Amherst Business Centre
Budbrooke Road
Warwick
CV34 5WE
England
Tel. 01926 499 619
Email: info@helion.co.uk
Website: www.helion.co.uk
Twitter: @helionbooks
https://helionbooks.wordpress.com/

Text © Andrey Latkin 2025
Photographs © as individually credited
Colour Profiles: Andrey Yurgenson

Designed and typeset by Mach 3 Solutions
(www.mach3solutions.co.uk)
Cover design Paul Hewitt, Battlefield Design
(www.battlefield-design.co.uk)

Every reasonable effort has been made to trace copyright holders and to obtain their permission for the use of copyright material. The author and publisher apologise for any errors or omissions in this work, and would be grateful if notified of any corrections that should be incorporated in future reprints or editions of this book.

ISBN: 978-1-804517-72-7

British Library Cataloguing-in-Publication Data
A catalogue record for this book is available
from the British Library

All rights reserved. No part of this publication may be reproduced, stored in a retrieval system, or transmitted, in any form, or by any means, electronic, mechanical, photocopying, recording or otherwise, without the express written consent of Helion & Company Limited.

We always welcome receiving book proposals from prospective authors.

I0869041

Note: In order to simplify the use of this book, all names, locations and geographic designations are as provided in *The Times World Atlas*, or other traditionally accepted major sources of reference, as of the time of described events.

ABBREVIATIONS AND ACRONYMS

GIAP – Guards Fighter Aviation Regiment (*Gvardeiskiy Istrebitelniy Aviatsionniy Polk*)
GKAP – Guards Red-Banner Aviation Regiment (*Gvardeiskiy Krasnoznamenniy Aviatsionniy Polk*)
GMTAP – Guards Mine-Torpedo Aviation Regiment (*Gvardeiskiy Minno-Torpedniy Aviatsionniy Polk*)
HQ – Headquarters
IAD – Fighter Aviation Division (*Istrebitelnaya Aviatsionnaya Diviziya*)
IAE – Fighter Aviation Squadron (*Istrebitelnaya Aviatsionnaya Eskadriliya*)
IAP – Fighter Aviation Regiment (*Istrebitelniy Aviatsionniy Polk*)
KFK – multi-purpose boat (*Kriegsfischkutter*)
MFP – naval ferry barge (*Marinefährprahm*)
MTAD – Mine-Torpedo Aviation Division (*Minno-Torpednaya Aviatsionnaya Diviziya*)
MTAP – Mine-Torpedo Aviation Regiment (*Minno-Torpedniy Aviatsionniy Polk*)
RAP – Reconnaissance Aviation Regiment (*Razvedyvatelniy Aviatsionniy Polk*)
SAD – Composite Aviation Division (*Smeshannaya Aviatsionnaya Diviziya*)
SAP – Composite Aviation Regiment (*Smeshanniy Aviatsionniy Polk*)
ShAP – Ground-attack Aviation Regiment (*Shturmovoy Aviatsionniy Polk*)

INTRODUCTION

Why this book was written? Well, the author simply got tired of reading the same stories over and over again – the stories put together by other authors about the combat use of Kittyhawk aircraft by the Northern Fleet Air Force. It seems that different authors have a lot to tell about the design of these aircraft, their deliveries under Lend-Lease agreement, but when it comes to combat use of the Kittyhawks, all authors write the same stories. So, the author, with the support of his friends, went to a branch office of the Central Archive of the Ministry of Defence of the Russian Federation (Archive of the Navy branch) in the town of Gatchina and found documents related to the combat use of this aircraft type in the Northern Fleet Air Force.

In the battles of 1942–1943 the Kittyhawks operated as fighters. That is why the author quoted the documents and combat flight logs of the pilots of the 2nd Guards Red-Banner Fighter Aviation Regiment named after B.F. Safonov with some additions taken from the documents of the Northern Fleet Air Force Headquarters. Anyway, who would better know all the difficulties of fighting enemy aircraft than the pilots themselves and their superiors? The author managed to find most of the confirmed air victories of the Kittyhawk pilots and the names of the pilots who won them. However, since wars always bring losses, the Kittyhawks missing in 1942–1944 are also included into this book.

From the end of 1943 the Kittyhawk aircraft, while keeping its fighter role, became more frequently used as a reconnaissance aircraft and a fighter-bomber. The latter was the most interesting topic to research, and the author was able to find a large number of pilots' reports, combat flight logs and gun camera photos of strikes which gave an idea of how the pilots and their commanders saw the course and outcome of a particular battle. Documents from the American NARA archives helped to show how the enemy saw the Kittyhawks attacking their ships and vessels, and also gave the results of these strikes. On the other hand, sometimes due to the lack of German documents, not all the ground target strikes are described, as in a number of cases the documents available to the author cannot give an answer about the effectiveness of those strikes.

The author would like to thank Igor Borisenko, Josef Falk, Hans-Ulrich Henschel, Andrey Kopytkov, Aleksander Mardanov, Vyacheslav Mosunov, Vladimir Nayavt, Gennady Sloutskiy, Yuriy Rybin, Pavel Vein and all the staff at the Central Archive of the Ministry of Defence of the Russian Federation (Archive of the Navy branch) for their considerable support in the creation of this book.

HISTORICAL NOTE: THE 2ND GUARDS RED-BANNER FIGHTER AVIATION REGIMENT NAMED AFTER B.F. SAFONOV

The regiment was formed in December 1939 as the 72nd Composite Aviation Regiment of the Northern Fleet Air Force. The regiment included both fighters and bombers, and later (in 1942) even torpedo bombers. In fact, this regiment became the progenitor of all the air forces of the Northern Fleet, being later transformed into two fighter and one mine-torpedo regiments.

On 22 June 1941 the regiment was commanded by Colonel G.P. Gubanov.

On 16 September 1941 the regiment was awarded the Order of the Red Banner.

On 18 January 1942 for success in battles with the enemy the regiment received the rank of Guards and was renamed into the 2nd Guards Red-Banner Composite Aviation Regiment.

On 15 June 1942 the regiment was named after B.F. Safonov, the regiment commander, who died in an air battle on 30 May 1942.

On 14 October 1942, after the withdrawal of bomber and mine-torpedo squadrons from the regiment (they were included into the 24th Mine-Torpedo Aviation Regiment, the future 9th Guards Mine-Torpedo Aviation Regiment), the regiment was renamed into the 2nd Guards Red-Banner Fighter Aviation Regiment named after B.F. Safonov.

The regiment took an active part in the battles of 1944, for which on 31 October 1944 it was awarded the honorary name 'Pechengskiy'.

1
KITTYHAWKS, JUNE 1944

The first month of the summer of 1944 was marked by the raids of attack aircraft and fighter-bombers on the port of Kirkenes. The Soviet Air Force became strong enough to strike Kirkenes in large numbers. The strikes damaged the port infrastructure, industrial and city facilities. This made it difficult to supply the German forces in the north and export the necessary raw materials for Nazi's industry.

In June 1944 the 27th and 78th IAPs carried out strikes on Kirkenes, with the Kittyhawks acting as fighter-bombers, i.e. after dropping the bombs they would push the Luftwaffe fighters out of the strike area.

The great contribution of the rear service in ensuring the strikes on Kirkenes should be noted. During the second quarter, 110 Kittyhawk aircraft were equipped with electrical wiring and pyrotechnic charges for dropping bombs. This made it possible to suspend two FAB-100s and one FAB-250 on each aircraft. In addition, the rear service bases began to convert the Kittyhawks to dual control, which greatly facilitated the training of flight crews.

In June 1944, the 27th IAP flew 257 combat missions, 26 of which were directed against ships and convoys. In addition to attacking ships, 12 missions were carried out to attack enemy bases. The regiment pilots shot down one Bf 109 without losing any of their aircraft during the month.

Despite the fact that the 78th IAP flew fewer combat missions, it was more often engaged in air combat and shot down more enemy aircraft. In June 1944, the 78th IAP flew 186 combat missions, 37 of which were against ships and convoys. The regiment flew 78 missions to strike enemy bases and 22 more to attack enemy artillery batteries. In the air battles, five Bf 109s and one FW 190 were claimed shot down. During the month the regiment suffered two losses: one Kittyhawk due to combat reasons and one for technical failure. The flight crews lost two pilots.

7 June

Four Kittyhawk fighter-bombers of the 78th IAP (leader – Senior Lieutenant A.I. Batrakov) took off on a 'free hunting' mission. From the combat flight log of 6th IAD:

"22:40. Ten kilometres to the north-west of Makkaur Cape the aircraft fired machine guns and then dropped bombs on two barges using the skip-bombing method from an altitude of 10–15m, distance 250–200m. Junior Lieutenant Proyavko sank one self-propelled barge with a direct hit of two FAB-100s. Senior Lieutenant Batrakov and Junior Lieutenant Shvailakh sank the second self-propelled barge by direct hit of bombs. The first barge had a displacement of 400–500 tonnes, the second – 300–400 tonnes."

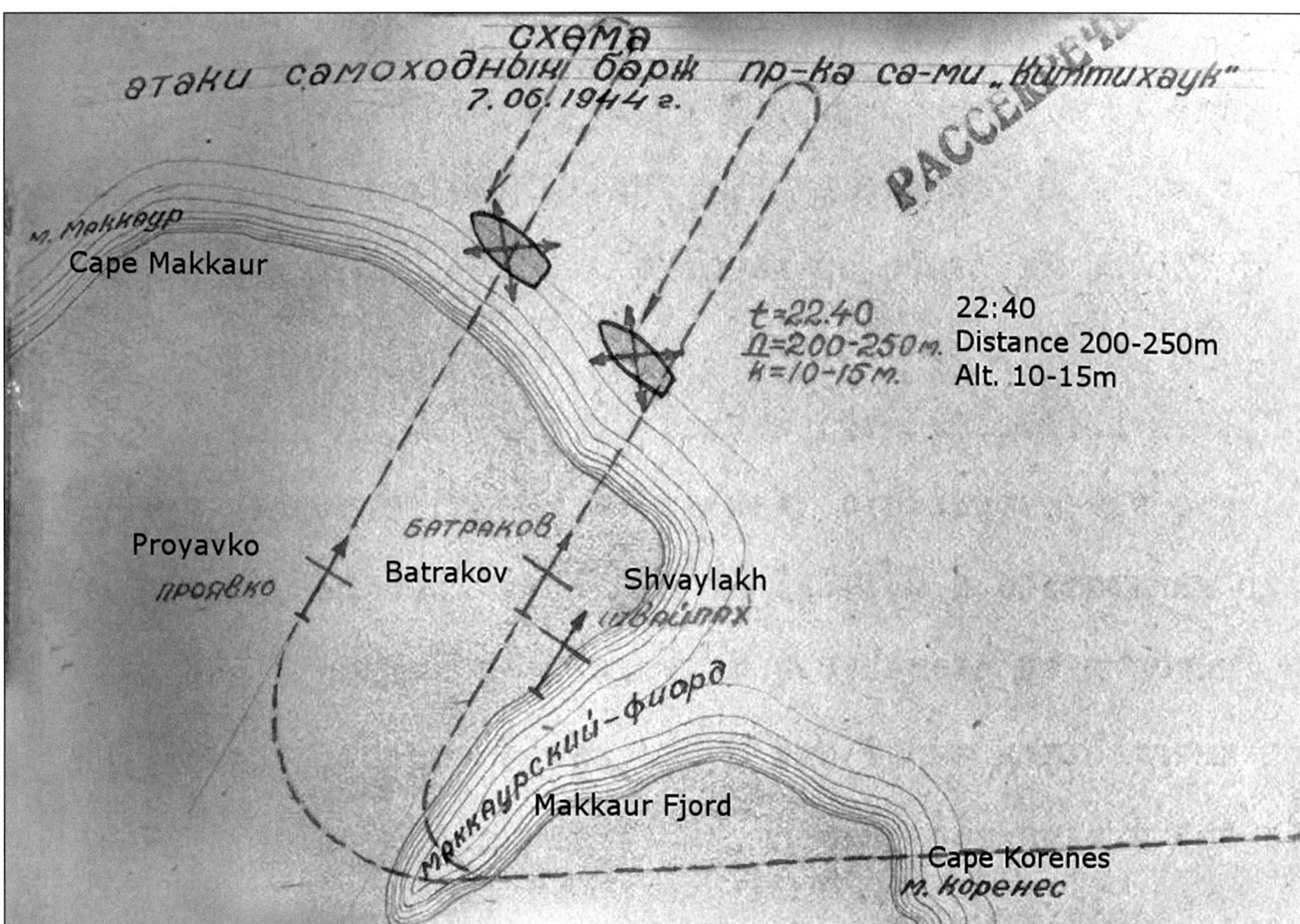

Plan of attack on the German motorboats by the 27th IAP Kittyhawks on 7 June 1944.

According to German documents, two motorboats were attacked off Makkaur Cape, one of them, the *T 52-T Polarfjell*, was damaged. One passenger was injured. During the attack, the Kittyhawk piloted by Junior Lieutenant N.P. Proyavko, hit the mast of the motorboat over the target. Despite serious damage to the aircraft, the pilot managed to reach his home base, flying almost two hundred kilometres. On landing, the damaged aircraft fell on the wing, the leg of the landing gear broke off, the gearbox came off. The aircraft was repaired and the pilot was not injured. A piece of the ship's mast stuck in the aircraft's wing was removed and sent as an exhibition in the Central Museum of the Navy, where it remains to this day.

13 June

An accident occurred in the 78th IAP – Junior Lieutenant I.P. Albul, while practicing at the training range, made a piloting mistake and crashed into the water. As a result, the aircraft was lost and the pilot died. It was a great loss for the regiment as Junior Lieutenant I.P. Albul took part in many combat sorties and managed to open his combat account in the battle against the German convoys by shooting down a Bf 109.

15 June

In the evening, Soviet aviation struck the port of Liinahamari. The attack was carried out by two groups of six Il-2s each of the 46th ShAP (leaders – Senior Lieutenant V.I. Belashev and Lieutenant N.N. Surovov) and eight Kittyhawk fighter-bombers of the 78th IAP (leader – Senior Lieutenant P.I. Sakharov) under cover of 10 Airacobras, eight Yak-7Bs and nine Yak-9s of the 20th IAP (leaders – Lieutenant K.V. Boychenko, Lieutenant L.P. Lapin, and Captain A.P. Shipov).The first to attack were the Kittyhawk fighter-bombers. From the combat flight log of the 6th IAD:

"20:04. The bombs were dropped from a dive, from an altitude of 800m, on the piers, warehouses and two boats, a phosphate factory and an anti-aircraft battery in the area of the port of Liinahamari. The strike destroyed one warehouse on the III-shaped pier. The phosphate factory was set on fire, the fuel depot was blown up, anti-aircraft battery fire was suppressed and two motorboats were damaged. Senior Lieutenants Sakharov, Strelnikov and Junior Lieutenant Venikov fired machine guns from an altitude of 200m at the enemy coastal battery. The results were not observed."

The Kittyhawks were followed by the attack aircraft of the 46th ShAP. At 20:10, the Il-2s attacked from a dive and struck the piers and warehouses in the port. Simultaneously with their attack, the port was fired at by coastal batteries of the Northern Defense Region from the Sredniy Peninsula. As a result of the air strike and fire of the coastal batteries on the port and the warehouses in Liinahamari, the Swedish Pier and the big barracks near it caught fire; a quantity of shells for anti-aircraft guns were destroyed as well. The fire caused an explosion of depth charges stored in the barracks, and burned the haystacks and sheds near the main pier.

After several hours of fighting the fires and clearing the aftermath of the attack, the Germans were able to assess the damage. It was extensive: eight barracks were destroyed or set on fire, including two with straw/hay and one with cement, and two other barracks were badly damaged. The motorboat *Elbe* was destroyed by fire, the motorboats *Nachteule* and *Jade* were badly damaged, the *Hamburg* lightly damaged. Of the two steamers at the Swedish Pier one managed to move away from the pier, while the other, the *Nerissa*, took a direct hit from a shell, which destroyed the deck derrick-crane. Ammunition for anti-tank and anti-aircraft guns, infantry weapons and depth charges stockpiled on the Swedish Pier were partially destroyed by explosions. About 300–400 people took part in the extinguishing of fires and rescue actions. The port communication system was knocked out of operation by the bomb explosions. Casualties amounted to one killed, seven wounded.

7./JG 5 flew out to intercept the Soviet aircraft. From the combat flight log of 6th IAD: "At 20:12, two Kittyhawks engaged in air combat with two Bf 109s near Volokovaya mountain, at an altitude of 200m. As a result of the air combat, Junior Lieutenant Venikov shot down one Bf 109, the aircraft went down near Trifon."

Based on the results of the air combat the Northern Fleet Air Force Headquarters credited one downed Bf 109 to Junior Lieutenant V.V. Venikov of the 78th IAP and one supposedly downed Bf 109 to Senior Lieutenant V.M. Shvechkov of the 20th IAP. German sources report nothing about losses of Luftwaffe fighters or their absence. The Luftwaffe fighter pilots credited 10 downed Soviet aircraft, and four more were claimed by anti-aircraft artillery gunners. In reality, all Soviet aircraft were able to return to their home airfields. The Germans drew conclusions from this raid and placed one more anti-aircraft *Vierling* gun in a position near the Liinahamari fuel tanks.

17 June

On this day another battle between the Northern Fleet Air Force and a German convoy took place. The convoy was spotted by a reconnaissance aircraft of the 118th RAP in the evening of 16 June and the command of the Northern Fleet Air Force began to plan an operation against it.

The convoy against which the attack was being prepared was Rp.121.Ki. It left Reppa Fjord on 15 June 1944 and was en route to Kirkenes. The convoy consisted of the floating base of the motor minesweepers *Weser*, minesweepers M-31, M-35, M-154, M-202, M-252, patrol ships V-6102, V-6107, V-6110, V-6111, V-6722, V-6725, submarine hunters UJ-1209, UJ-1211, UJ-1212, UJ-1219, UJ-1220, motor minesweepers R-160, R-202, R-223, R-301, R-304, R-307, R-308, steamers *Florianopolis* (7,419grt), *Herm Fritzen* (3,845grt), *William Blumer* (3,604grt), *Margarethe Cords* (1,912grt), *Iris* (3,323grt), *Dixie* (1,571grt), *Transport* (1,998grt), *Feiestein* (461grt), tankers *Tripp* (364grt) and *Algol* (972grt).

The command post of the Northern Fleet Air Force started planning the attack on the convoy. It was decided to strike at it in the morning of 17 June 1944, in the vicinity of Kibergnes. Almost all available forces of the Northern Fleet Air Force were to take part in the operation. The Kittyhawk fighter-bombers were the first to attack, striking the German escort ships. In addition to this strike, six Kittyhawks were to drop smoke bombs to interfere with the anti-aircraft artillery and ensure the strike of the attack aircraft and torpedo bombers. Fighter cover for the Kittyhawks was to be provided by Airacobras of the 2nd GKAP. The convoy was then to be attacked by two groups of high-altitude torpedo bombers and three groups of attack aircraft covered by fighters.

At 5:25, a Kittyhawk reconnaissance aircraft of the 118th RAP, piloted by Junior Lieutenant I.P. Mashkov, completed the reconnaissance task of the convoy in the Hamningberg area.

Twelve Kittyhawk fighter-bombers of the 78th IAP (leader – Captain D.I. Sinev) and eight Kittyhawk fighter-bombers of the 27th IAP (leader – Senior Lieutenant A.P. Anuchin) flew first, as planned, under the cover of 10 Airacobras of the 2nd GKAP (leader – Guards Major D.F. Marenko). Captain D.I. Sinev carried out overall leadership of all aircraft in the group. Not all of the aircraft reached the target – three Kittyhawks had to return. The aircraft which were flown by Lieutenant N.M. Ivanov of the 27th IAP and Lieutenant V.G. Mitrofanov of the 78th IAP had engine troubles, while Lieutenant D.P. Dzyuba covered their return.

At 8:42, Kittyhawk fighter-bombers attacked the convoy from a dive near Kibergnes. From the combat flight log of the 6th IAD:

> At 8:42, four Kittyhawks, led by Lieutenant Sakharov, dropped eight FAB-100s from a dive at an altitude of 800m on the enemy ships and transports. The direct hit by the bomb dropped by Senior Lieutenant Strelnikov damaged the patrol boat. Two Kittyhawks, while approaching the target, were attacked by two Bf 109s, four FAB-100 bombs were dropped on the convoy without aiming. Six Kittyhawks, led by Captain Sinev, dropped 12 DAB-100 smoke bombs on the course of the convoy to the right, smoke screen was not effective.

The combat log of 12th Submarine Hunters Flotilla records that UJ-1209, UJ-1219, and UJ-1220 were attacked. The attack on UJ-1209 resulted in a damaged pipe and stern raft. A bag of emergency provisions attached to it caught fire, but was quickly extinguished.

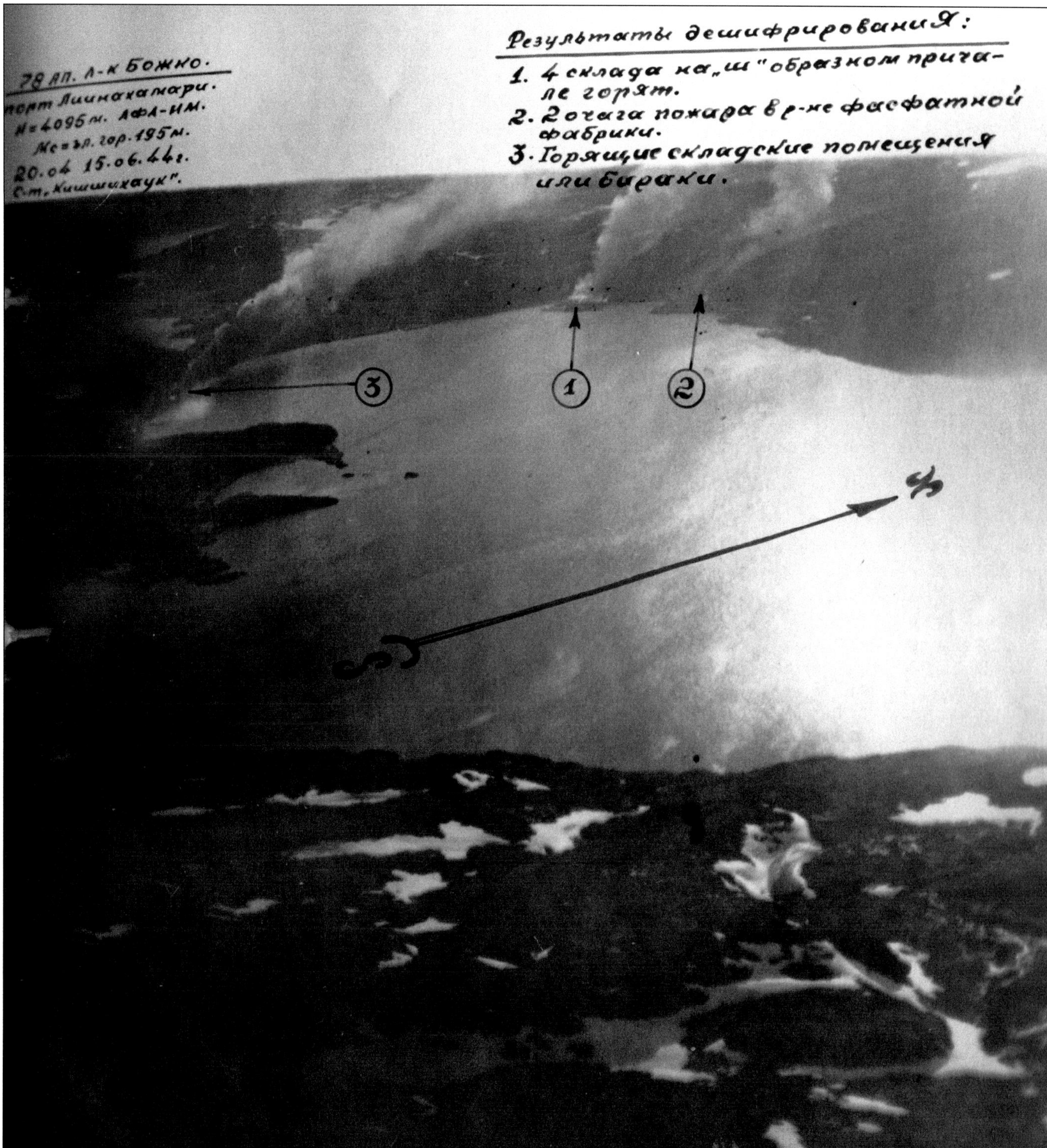

Photo reconnaissance report of the results of the air strike on Liinahamari, 15 June 1944.
78th IAP, pilot Bozhko; Port Liinahamari; Altitude 4,095m; AFA-IM camera; 20:04 15 June 1944; Kittyhawk aircraft.
Results of the photo reconnaissance interpretation: 1. Four warehouses at the Ш-shaped pier are on fire; 2. Two spots of fire at the area of the phosphate factory; 3. Warehouses or barracks on fire.

Twelve minutes later, at 8:54, the Kittyhawks of the 27th IAP launched their attack. From the combat flight log of the 6th IAD: "At 8:54, bombs were dropped from a dive, from an altitude of 1,000–800m on the ships and transports of the convoy in the area of Kibergnes. As a result of the attack, bomb hits were noticed within 20–30 m from the transports and ships of the convoy." The German anti-aircraft gunners fired quite accurately: three Kittyhawks, piloted by Senior Lieutenant A.P. Anuchin, Lieutenant P.M. Demikov, and Junior Lieutenant I.Yu. Panov, were damaged by anti-aircraft fire. Above the convoy, the Airacobras and Kittyhawks were engaged in several air battles against Luftwaffe fighters and a hydroplane. From the combat flight log of the 6th IAD (report of pilots of the 78th IAP):

> At 8:55, the pilots were engaged in air combat against eight Bf 109s in the area of the convoy at an altitude of 600–1,200m. As a result of the air engagement, Senior Lieutenant Strelnikov shot down one Bf 109, the enemy aircraft came down in the convoy area. Junior Lieutenant Kulikov shot down one Bf 109, the enemy aircraft fell down in the convoy area. Junior Lieutenant Nerubenko supposedly shot down one Bf 109, the enemy aircraft crashed in the convoy area.

Pilots of the 27th IAP reported the following:

> At 8:53–8:58, while approaching the target, four Kittyhawks were engaged in an air combat against five Bf 109s over the target and on the withdrawal, at an altitude of 600–800m. As a result of the combat, Junior Lieutenant Demikov shot down one Bf 109, the enemy aircraft came down two kilometres to the east of the convoy.

Based on the results of the air battle, the Headquarters of the Northern Fleet Air Force credited Captain V.P. Maksimovich, Senior Lieutenants N.A. Bokiy and N.M. Didenko of the 2nd GKAP, Senior Lieutenant V.P. Strelnikov of the 78th IAP, Junior Lieutenant P.M. Demikov of the 27th IAP, and Junior Lieutenants I.G. Kulikov and N.A. Nerubenko of the 78th IAP one downed Bf 109 each. One Do 24 hydroplane was credited to the pilots of the 2nd GKAP, but, judging by German documents, this aircraft, though damaged, managed to reach its home airfield.

Three groups of attack aircraft followed the fighter-bombers. The first group consisted of six Il-2s of the 46th ShAP (leader – Captain A.N. Sinitsyn), four Yak fighters of the 20th IAP (leader – Lieutenant L.P. Lapin) and six Airacobras of the 20th IAP (leader – Lieutenant N.D. Tkachenko). At 9:04, the attack aircraft struck the convoy from a dive, from the stern of the convoy, with the task of suppressing the anti-aircraft fire of the German escort ships. According to German data, a group of attack aircraft struck the floating base *Weser* and the patrol ship V-6722, but all the bombs missed them. This group was able to divert the attention of some of the convoy's anti-aircraft guns and facilitate the attack of the strike groups following it. Anti-aircraft artillery of the convoy shot down two attack aircraft, and their crews were killed. Above the target, the attack aircraft were engaged by four Bf 109s, but the escort fighters repulsed the attack.

The second group of attack aircraft consisted of six Il-2s of the 46th ShAP (leader – Captain S.A. Gulyaev) and 10 Airacobras of the 20th IAP (leader – Senior Lieutenant A.K. Tarasov). At 9:07, the attack aircraft dropped their FAB-250s onto the enemy transports which were in the rear of the convoy. The Il-2s succeeded in hitting the steamship *Florianopolis* (6,062grt) with one FAB-250. The bomb hit the bow of the steamship, but the crew managed to extinguish the fire and the ship, having separated from the convoy, reached Kirkenes under escort of five motor minesweepers. Two attack aircraft were shot down by anti-aircraft artillery over the target, their crews were killed. During the retreat from the target, the group of attack aircraft was intercepted by six Luftwaffe fighters. The pilots of the 20th IAP claimed two victories over Luftwaffe, and the navigator of one of the attack aircraft claimed one more kill.

The last, third, group of attack aircraft, started the strike at the same time as the second group. The group included four Il-2s (leader – Senior Lieutenant V.I. Belashev), four Yaks of the 20th IAP (leader – Lieutenant I.P. Kuzhanov) and four Airacobras of the 20th IAP (leader – Lieutenant I.V. Logutov). At 9:07 the attack aircraft dropped their bombs on the transports. The target was the second from the end transport of the convoy, probably the floating base *Weser*. After dropping bombs on the transport, on the way out of the attack the Il-2s fired machine guns and cannon at the submarine hunter UJ-1209. Fire broke out on the vessel, and eight of the ship's crew, including the commander, were wounded.

At 9:07, a group of high-altitude torpedo bombers consisting of four Il-4s of the 9th GMTAP (leader – Guards Major A.N. Voloshin) under cover of four Airacobras of the 255th IAP and eight Kittyhawks of the 78th IAP (leader – Major A.V. Polkovnikov) attacked the convoy. They dropped four torpedoes into the gap in the clouds and observed a hit. The group had no encounters with Luftwaffe fighters.

At 9:08, a group of six Bostons of the 9th GMTAP (leader – Guards Lieutenant Colonel S.K. Litvinov) under the cover of 16 Airacobras of the 255th IAP (leader – Captain P.A. Rassadkin) attacked the convoy. After dropping six torpedoes into the gap in the clouds, the group watched them hit a ship. The escort fighters repulsed an attack by six Luftwaffe fighters, shooting down one Bf 109 and damaging one of them.

The attack by two groups of torpedo bombers resulted in one torpedo hitting the steamer *Dixie* (1,571grt) which quickly sank.

The German side participated in the air battle with Bf 109s of *Stab* III./JG 5, and the 7., 8., and 9. *Staffeln* of the JG 5. In all, Luftwaffe fighters flew 25 combat missions to defend the convoy and claimed 35 victories over the Soviet aircraft, three more were claimed by the anti-aircraft artillery gunners of the convoy ships, and two by the Battery *Kiberg*. The actual Soviet losses amounted to four attack aircraft, though, according to Soviet records, all from anti-aircraft fire. According to the currently available data, one Luftwaffe fighter was badly damaged in combat over the convoy and crashed during the forced landing at Kiberg. It was Bf 109G-6, W.Nr. 411071, tactical number 'White 4', of the 7./JG 5. Its pilot, *Unteroffizier* Josef Suske, was wounded.

The Northern Fleet Air Force command took measures to search for the crews of the downed attack aircraft. However, all the efforts made by the torpedo boats and the Catalina aircraft failed.

After suffering losses, Convoy Rp.121.Ki reached Kirkenes. However, the Northern Fleet Air Force command did not hesitate to attack the convoy again in the port of Kirkenes. In addition to ships and vessels, the attack was to target the port and warehouses, as well as the ore processing plant.

The Kittyhawks were assigned the following tasks:

a) Twenty-six fighter-bombers of the 78th and 27th IAPs were to bomb the port and warehouses in the north-eastern part of the town. After dropping the bombs, they were to patrol over the city to provide fighter cover for other groups.
b) Six fighter-bombers of the 27th IAP together with four Il-4 bombers were to drop bombs on the central part of

the town with the task of destroying warehouses and residential buildings.

At 18:00, the commanders of the units and formations were summoned to the command post of the Northern Fleet Air Force to receive orders for the operation. The order of action for the groups was worked out and the targets were distributed. The time of the strike was set for 22:00.

At exactly 22:00, 18 Airacobras of the 2nd GKAP (leader – Guards Major I.M. Sukhomlin) appeared over Kirkenes. The task of the group was to drive Luftwaffe fighters out of the attack area.

Luftwaffe fighters appeared twenty minutes later. Twelve Bf 109s engaged in air combat against Airacobras of the 2nd GKAP, during which Guards Senior Lieutenants N.A. Bokiy, N.M. Didenko and Guards Lieutenant E.I. Gredyushko shot down one Luftwaffe fighter each. Soviet fighters sustained no losses.

After the Airacobras, 25 Kittyhawk fighter-bombers appeared over Kirkenes. All aircraft, except two equipped with photo cameras, carried one FAB-250 high-explosive bomb and two FAB-100TsK incendiary bombs each.

According to the plan, there were to be 26 Kittyhawks: 20 of the 78th IAP (leader – Major V.I. Babernov) and six of the 27th IAP (leader – Captain Yu.Kh. Gryaznov). On approach to the target, the aircraft flown by the group commander, Major V.I. Babernov, began experiencing engine problems. Having handed over command to his deputy, Captain D.I. Sinev, he returned to the Vaenga-2 airfield.

The aircraft of the 78th IAP were the first to attack. From the combat flight log of the 6th IAD: "Between 22:02 and 22:05, the aircraft dropped bombs from an altitude of 1,500m on the north-west part of the town of Kirkenes. As a result of the attack, eight to ten fires started in the town and ore processing plant, the bombs exploded in the area of the warehouses and the port mooring." During the attack, anti-aircraft artillery shot down one Kittyhawk of the 78th IAP. From the accident report on the loss of the Kittyhawk aircraft: "The aircraft was fired upon by anti-aircraft artillery in the target area and, as a result of a direct hit, the aircraft of Junior Lieutenant Logutov was shot down." Junior Lieutenant I.G. Logutov was taken prisoner.

The aircraft of 27th IAP attacked next. From the combat flight log of the 6th IAD: "At 22:15, the aircraft dropped bombs from a dive, from an altitude of 1,500m, on the north-west part of the city. As a result of the strike, two fires were seen in the ore processing plant. One anti-aircraft battery of the enemy was suppressed by a direct bomb hit." After dropping the bombs, the Kittyhawks, together with the Airacobras of the 2nd GKAP, patrolled over Kirkenes and engaged in air combat with Luftwaffe fighters.

From the combat flight log of the 6th IAD: "At 22:08, eight Kittyhawks were engaged in air combat in the target area at an altitude of 2,500–1,800m against six Bf 109s without success. At 22:11, on withdrawal, at 1,800m altitude, the aircraft were engaged in air combat against two FW 190s. As a result, Lieutenant Lisichkin shot down one FW 190, the enemy's aircraft came down in the area of Poura-Nuono." As the result of the air combat the Northern Fleet Air Force Headquarters credited one downed FW 190 to the pilot of 78th IAP Junior Lieutenant N.R. Lisichkin.

At 22:08, the group of attack aircraft of the 46th ShAP followed the fighter-bombers. It consisted of six Il-2s (leader – Lieutenant V.I. Belashev) and 10 Airacobras of the 20th IAP (leader – Lieutenant K.V. Boychenko). The attacking aircraft dropped bombs from a dive in the north-west part of the city on the port, warehouses and residential buildings. The attack resulted in fires in the city and port. Several attack aircraft struck the ships and vessels in the port following the orders of the leader. As a result of their attack, the steamer *Margareta Cords* (1,912grt) with its cargo of collapsible barracks caught fire. The fire was extinguished by the Germans, and on 9 July 1944 the ship departed from Beck Fjord with a convoy. In addition to the *Margareta Cords*, the motor minesweeper R-154 was hit by machine-gun fire in the harbour of Kirkenes. One crew member was wounded. While retreating from the target, the group engaged Luftwaffe fighters. Following the results of the air battle, the Northern Fleet Air Force Headquarters credited one downed Bf 109 to the pilots of the 20th IAP, Senior Lieutenant A.K. Tarasov and Lieutenant G.I. Dymovskiy each.

The group of Lieutenant V.I. Belashev lost one Il-2 and one Airacobra. The crew of the attack aircraft were taken prisoner, and the fighter pilot was killed.

Simultaneously with Balashev's group, another group of attack aircraft carried out a discharge of granulated phosphorus over the target. The group included four Il-2s (leader – Senior Lieutenant N.N. Surovov) and 10 Yak-7Bs of the 20th IAP (leader – Captain A.A. Malinovskiy). The attack aircraft struck Kirkenes, passing from west to east along the southern part of the town, discharging the granulated phosphorus. As a result, the crews observed a continuous line of fire and smoke in the southern part of the town along the course of the aircraft. Anti-aircraft artillery shot down one attack aircraft, its pilot was killed and the air gunner was taken prisoner.

Luftwaffe fighters attacked the Il-2s after the phosphorous discharge, but they were repelled by the escort fighters.

Three groups of bombers of the 5th MTAD followed the attackers.

The first group consisted of five Bostons of the 36th MTAP (leader – Captain G.P. Khamkov) under the cover of 10 Airacobras of the 20th IAP (leader – Lieutenant N.D. Tkachenko). At 22:14, they dropped FAB-500 bombs on the north-eastern part of the city and observed several fires caused by the explosions.

The second group consisted of four Il-4s of the 9th GMTAP (leader – Guards Major A.N. Voloshin), six Kittyhawk fighter-bombers of the 27th IAP (leader – Senior Lieutenant A.P. Anuchin) and six Airacobras of the 255th IAP (leader – Captain F.E. Samarkov). One minute after the aircraft of the 36th MTAP, Il-4 bombers struck the centre of Kirkenes, where explosions and fires were observed. At the same time, the Kittyhawks, which were part of the group, dropped two FAB-100s dive bombs each on the power station.

The last to drop their bombs on Kirkenes were six Bostons of the 9th GMTAP (leader – Guards Lieutenant Colonel S.K. Litvinov) under the cover of 12 Airacobras of the 255th IAP (leader – Captain P.A. Rassadkin). The targets for the Bostons were residential and warehouse buildings in the eastern part of the city, and, according to the crews' observations, fires broke out there. In addition, the group observed the steamer *Margareta Cords* burning in the harbour, which had been damaged by the attack aircraft.

The third group, the only one of the three bomber groups in the air raid, was attacked by individual Luftwaffe fighters. The Germans achieved nothing, while basing on the results of the air battle, the Northern Fleet Air Force Headquarters credited one downed FW 190 to Junior Lieutenant V.I. Bukanov of the 255th IAP.

The strike force was followed by a Spitfire reconnaissance aircraft of the 118th RAP piloted by Junior Lieutenant K.V. Popovich. Excellent British cameras captured the results of the attack perfectly.

According to German reports, the incendiary bombs caused many fires which were extinguished with great difficulty. Eight Wehrmacht barracks and eight Norwegian residential buildings were burned down, and 60 percent of the electrical wires had to be replaced. The Wehrmacht wrote off two motor vehicles, with two more going into repairs. Many German soldiers and officers were wounded, and six Norwegians were injured.

Luftwaffe fighters of the 7. and 8. *Staffeln* and the *Stab* III./JG 5 flew to intercept Soviet aircraft during the attack on Kirkenes. In all, they claimed 27 victories over Soviet aircraft while losing one of their own. The German anti-aircraft artillery gunners sincerely believed that they had shot down eight more Soviet aircraft. In fact, four Soviet aircraft did not return from this mission, shot down either by fighters or by anti-aircraft fire. Soviet fighters reported seven victories over Luftwaffe. German documents confirm only one loss: Bf 109G-6, tactical number 'White 5', W.Nr. 411463, of the 7./JG 5. Its pilot, *Obfhr.* Hans Vollet, was wounded but managed to bail out with parachute.

Kittyhawks at the airfield.

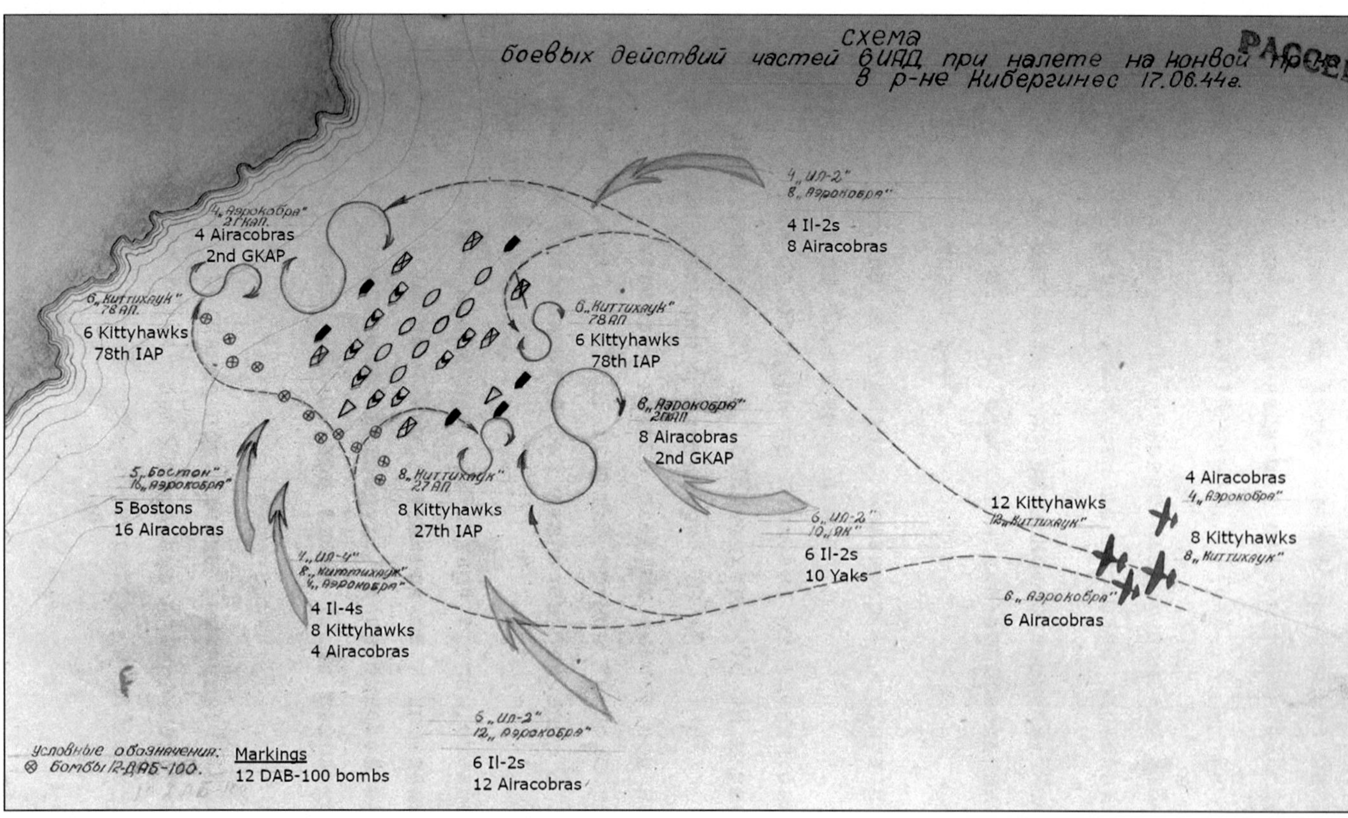

Plan of attack on the Rp.121.Ki convoy by Kittyhawks of the 27th and 78th IAPs on 17 June 1944.

22 June

At 23:21 four Kittyhawks of the 78th IAP (leader – Lieutenant A.J. Shvailakh) flew out for a 'free hunting' mission along the coast of Northern Norway. Three of them carried bombs and the fourth one was a photo reconnaissance aircraft, carrying camera for monitoring the results. About midnight, the fighter-bombers spotted a group of four high-speed landing barges AF-36, AF-39, F-197, and F-201. From the combat flight log of the 6th IAD: "The aircraft fired machine guns at four self-propelled barges of the enemy in the area of Korenes from an altitude of 300–500m, and three Kittyhawks struck using the skip-bombing method from an altitude of 20–30m, at distance of 250m. During the attack, the aircraft were exposed to anti-aircraft artillery and machine-gun fire." As a result of the attack, judging by German documents, no bombs hit high-speed landing barges, but there were seven wounded crewmen from machine-gun fire on the AF-39. The artillery barge had to return to Vardö to take them to hospital. The sailors of the AF-39 reported that they had shot down one Il-2, which crashed into the sea witnessed by the sailors. In fact, only two Kittyhawks were damaged. The Kittyhawk, piloted by Lieutenant A.Ya. Shvailakh, was damaged by direct hits by anti-artillery shells in its two machine guns in the left wing. The second Kittyhawk, piloted by Junior Lieutenant N.P. Proyavko, sustained damage to the fuselage from the anti-aircraft artillery and machine-gun fire. The damage from anti-aircraft fire did not prevent the two Kittyhawks from landing at 0:55 at their home airfield, where they were repaired by the technicians of the regiment.

23 June

After the first attack on four German barges, the command of the 6th IAD decided to launch a second strike and finish off the German ships. At 4:07, eight Kittyhawk fighter-bombers of the 78th IAP (leader – Captain V.P. Strelnikov) took off from Vaenga-2 airfield, followed by their escort fighters – six Airacobras of the 2nd GKAP (leader – Guards Captain S.M. Loginov).

At about 5:00, Soviet aircraft spotted AF-36, F-197, and F-201 in Kongs Fjord and attacked them. From the combat flight log of 6th IAD:

> 5:03. Flying at an altitude of 300–350 m, seven Kittyhawks dropped bombs on three self-propelled barges in the area of Kongs Fjord. As a result of a direct hit, Junior Lieutenant Volkov sank one self-propelled barge with a displacement of 1,200–1,500 tonnes. After the bomb strike, the aircraft fired at the barges loaded with soldiers, from a low altitude. In the target area, the aircraft were fired at by the enemy's anti-aircraft artillery.

Anti-aircraft gunners of German ships were firing quite accurately and were able to damage the Kittyhawk which was piloted by Junior Lieutenant I.G. Kulikov.

Above the target, the Soviet aircraft were attacked by Bf 109s of 8./JG 5. Pilots of the 78th IAP were the first to engage in the air battle. From the combat flight log of the 6th ID: "At 5:05, at 200–400m over the target, two Kittyhawks were engaged in air combat against four Bf

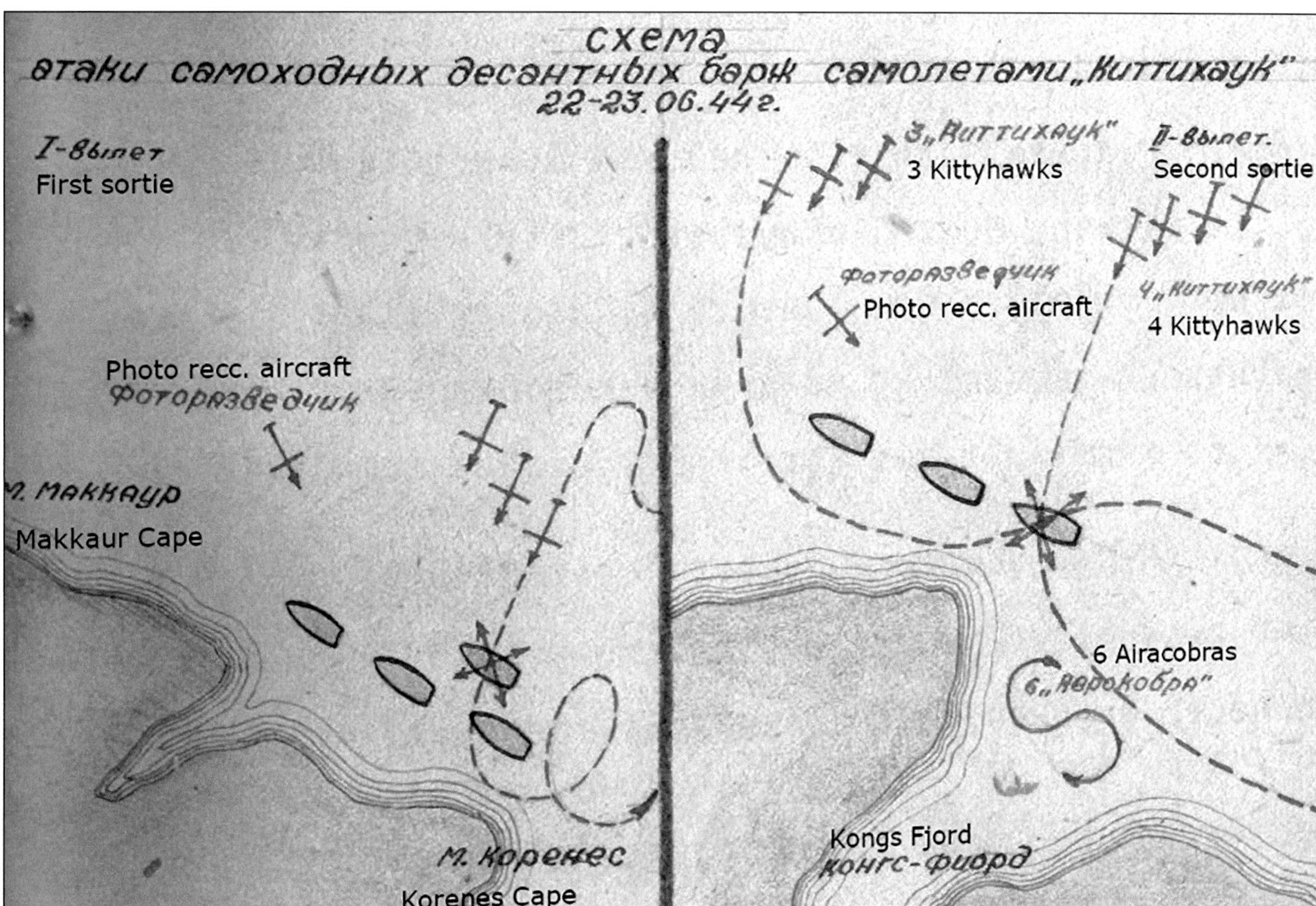

Plan of the Kittyhawks' attack on the German high-speed landing barges, 22–23 June 1944.

109s. As a result of the combat, Junior Lieutenant Kulikov supposedly shot down one Bf 109, which came down near Kongs Fjord."

Airacobras of the 2nd GKAP followed in the battle. From the combat flight log of the 6th IAD:

> At 5:05, in the area of Kongs Fjord, when moving away from the target at an altitude of 300m, the aircraft were engaged in an air combat against four Bf 109s and two FW 190s. As a result of the air combat Junior Lieutenant Borzystiy shot down one Bf 109; the aircraft crashed in the area of Haningsberg [Hamningberg – *Author's note*]. Lieutenant Zapalenov shot down one Bf 109, which crashed near Vardö. Guards Captain Loginov presumably shot down one FW 190 which fell east of Makkaur Cape.

Based on the results of the air battle, the Northern Fleet Air Force Headquarters credited one downed Bf 109 to Lieutenant N.I. Zapalenov and Lieutenant M.E. Borzystiy of the 2nd GKAP each, and one presumably downed Bf 109 was credited to Captain S.M. Loginov of the 2nd GKAP and Junior Lieutenant I.G. Kulikov of the 78th IAP each. The Luftwaffe pilots claimed three victories over Soviet aircraft but actually shot down one Airacobra of the 2nd GKAP, its pilot, Guards Lieutenant M.P. Glukhov, was killed.

27 June

On that day, the Northern Fleet Air Force Headquarters decided to repeat the strike on Kirkenes. The reason was a large number of targets, the destruction of which would cause great damage to German industry and forces.

The main target was the ore processing plant, warehouses with ore and military equipment for the German troops on the northern section of the Soviet-German front. The ships and vessels moored in the port of Kirkenes were also taken into consideration. Therefore, when weather conditions allowed for a massive attack on Kirkenes, it was carried out. The plan of the Northern Fleet Air Force command was to cause maximum damage to the port facilities, industry and infrastructure of the city and port by massive strikes to be carried out bomber and attack aircraft. The ships in the port were to be attacked simultaneously.

Eight Airacobras of the 2nd GKAP (leader – Lieutenant Colonel M.V. Semenikhin) and 20 Kittyhawk fighter-bombers of the 78th IAP (leader – Major V.I. Babernov) were the first to appear over Kirkenes. The group approached the target from the east, and at 17:45 the Kittyhawks dropped bombs on targets in the city. From the combat flight log of the 6th IAD:

> At 17:45, flying at a 20 degrees pitch angle at an altitude of 3,000m, the aircraft dropped one FAB-250 each, and then dived from an altitude of 1,500–1,000m and dropped two ZAB-100-TsKs each. As a result of the strike, four fires were noted in the central and southern parts of the city and in the north-western part of the city. The aircraft were subjected to heavy anti-aircraft artillery fire over the target area.

After dropping the bombs, the Kittyhawks joined the Airacobras of the 2nd GKAP and patrolled over Kirkenes to 'sweep out' the Luftwaffe fighters. During the patrols they engaged in several air combats against the enemy. From the combat flight log of the 6th IAD:

> At 17:55, east of the city of Kirkenes, at an altitude of 1,500m, eight Kittyhawks engaged in air combat against two Bf 109s. As a result of the air combat, Junior Lieutenant Venikov shot down one Bf 109, which fell six to five kilometres south of Kirkenes city. At 18:12, in the area of Volokovaya Mountain, at an altitude of 800m, two Kittyhawks fought an air battle against two Bf 109s without any results.

Basing on the results of the air combats, the Northern Fleet Air Force Headquarters credited one downed Bf 109 each to Lieutenant M.M. Chepurnov of the 2nd GKAP and Junior Lieutenant V.B. Venikov of the 78th IAP. On the return route, one Kittyhawk, piloted by Lieutenant V.P. Ivanov, was forced to land at Pummanki due to engine trouble.

After the fighter-bombers, bombs were dropped on Kirkenes by ground attack aircraft of the 46th ShAP. This group consisted of eight Il-2s (leader – Captain A.N. Sinitsyn) covered by twelve Airacobras of the 20th IAP (leader – Captain E.V. Petrenko) and four Yak-7Bs of the 20th IAP (leader – Lieutenant N.S. Zimin). At 17:50, the attack aircraft dropped FAB-250 bombs and launched rocket projectiles from a dive on the north-eastern part of the city. The crews reported explosions and fires in the town and at the ore processing plant. Luftwaffe fighters attempted to attack the groups on their withdrawal from the target, but the fighters and air gunners repulsed the attack, with one Bf 109 shot down by the air gunner of the 46th ShAP and another recorded as a group victory by the pilots of the 20th IAP.

After the strike by attack aircraft, bombs were dropped by the heavy fighters. The group included eight Pe-3s with bombs of the 95th IAP (leader – Major B.G. Khamdokhov) under cover of eight Airacobras of the 20th IAP (leader – Captain N.D. Tkachenko) and four Yak-7Bs of the 20th IAP (leader – Captain A.A. Malinovskiy). At 17:54, Pe-3s dropped bombs from a horizontal flight over the centre and the northern part of the city. The pilots reported explosions and fires in the areas where the bombs fell. While moving away from the target, two Yak-7Bs spotted a lone Bf 109 and Captain N.K. Kurenok shot it down.

Following the heavy fighters, four groups of Bostons of the 5th MTAD dropped bombs on Kirkenes. Their main targets were the ore processing plant, the piers and the ships in the port. The first of the attacking groups of Bostons consisted of five Bostons of the 9th MTAD (leader – Guards Lieutenant Colonel S.K. Litvinov) and 10 Airacobras of the 2nd GKAP (leader – Guards Captain I.M. Sukhomlin). At 17:55, their bombs fell on the north-western part of the city. In the report about the attack, the pilots noted five explosions and fires in the port area. The second group of bombers consisted of five Bostons of the 36th MTAP (leader – Major P.N. Obukhov) and eight Airacobras of the 255th IAP (leader – Major A.E. Tulskiy). At 17:55, the Bostons dropped FAB-1000 bombs on the north-western part of the city. The crews reported one bomb hitting the ore processing plant and another hitting the north-west pier. The fighters of the cover were engaged in several air combats during which they shot down a Bf 109. However, one Airacobra did not return from the combat mission. Its pilot, Junior Lieutenant I.N. Voronin, was killed.

The third bomber group consisted of five Bostons of the 36th MTAP (leader – Captain I.I. Ilyushin) and was covered by eight Airacobras of the 255th IAP (leader – Captain P. Rassadkin). One Airacobra failed to reach the target; it developed engine trouble and turned home. The aircraft failed to reach its home airfield, and ditched in the Kola Bay. Fortunately, the pilot was rescued by boats. At 17:56, the Bostons dropped bombs on the north-western part of the city. The crews reported five fires caused by their bombs.

The fourth bomber group consisted of five Bostons of the 36th MTAP (leader – Captain G.P. Khamkov) and eight Airacobras of

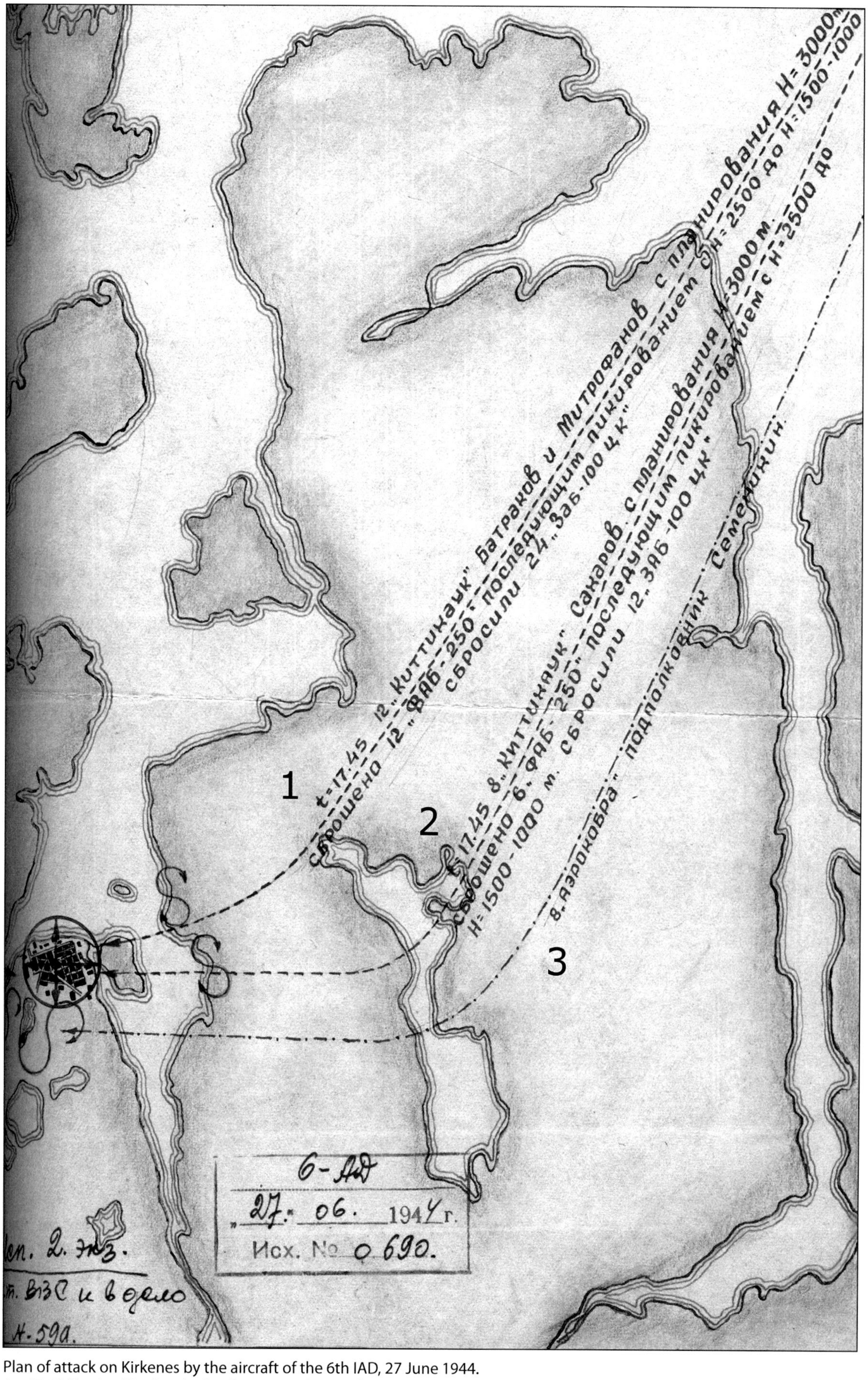

Plan of attack on Kirkenes by the aircraft of the 6th IAD, 27 June 1944.
1 – 17:45. Twelve Kittyhawks (leaders – Batrakov and Mitrofanov) dropped 12 FAB-250s from horizontal flight at an altitude of 3,000m, with a further dive from altitude of 2,500m to altitude of 1,500–1,000m dropping 24 ZAB-100TsK bombs.
2 – 17:45. Eight Kittyhawks (leader – Sakharov) dropped 6 FAB-250s from horizontal flight at an altitude of 3,000m, with a further dive from an altitude of 2,500m to altitude of 1,500–1,000m dropping 12 ZAB-100TsK bombs.
3 – Eight Airacobras led by Lieutenant Colonel Semenikhin.

the 255th IAP (leader – Captain F.E. Samarkov). At 17:56, the group dropped bombs on the facilities in the north-western part of the port. The crews of the group reported sinking and damaging several German ships. German documents say that several German ships were damaged by the close explosions. The most serious hit was sustained by the patrol ship V-6111. Two men were killed on it and 12 more were injured, three of them severely. The patrol boats NKi-23 (KFK.105) and NKi-14 (KFK.209) were sent for repairs due to nearby bomb explosions. The high-speed landing barge F-175 and patrol boat NKi-15 (KFK.210) sustained light damage according to German records. There were personnel losses on the patrol boats and high-speed landing barge, the number of which has not been established to date.

A reconnaissance aircraft of the 118th RAP, flying in to photograph the strike, reported: "The whole town is shrouded in smoke". German documents fully confirm this – the bombs hit the South Varanger factory, causing a fire there, and the railway tracks and the highway approaching it. The bombs also hit the headquarters of the naval defence commander, the communication stations, the naval barracks, and civilian houses. German military casualties were low, with only 10 men wounded.

28 June

After the strike on the evening of 27 June, the Northern Fleet Air Force command decided to repeat the attack on Kirkenes. The reason for this was the German ships. After the attack on Kirkenes, the reconnaissance aircraft spotted German ships approaching the island of Renö, moreover, a large number of German ships were anchored in Lang Fjord and at the piers of the port of Kirkenes. Immediately after landing of the strike groups, at 19:00 on 27 June, Northern Fleet Air Force Headquarters began to prepare a second attack on Kirkenes. The main task of the attack for all groups of bombers and attack aircraft was to hit the concentration of ships in Lang Fjord. In the absence of the latter, they were to hit the northern and north-eastern part of the town and the port.

At 1:02, 20 Kittyhawk fighter-bombers of the 78th IAP (leader – Captain D.I. Sinev) and 12 Airacobras of the 2nd GKAP (leader – Guards Major D.F. Marenko) were the first to appear over Kirkenes. At 1:05 the fighter-bombers attacked the targets in Kirkenes. From the combat flight log of the 6th IAD:

> Bombs were dropped from the horizontal flight and from a dive, from an altitude of 3,000–1,500m, on the central part of the city of Kirkenes. Four explosions were noted, the city wharf was damaged, one transport ship of 3,000 tonnes displacement was destroyed by a direct hit, two fires were observed. Four Kittyhawks dropped four FAB-250 bombs on the enemy convoy in the Jar Fjord, from 2,000m altitude, from horizontal flight. No results were observed. The aircraft sustained heavy anti-aircraft artillery fire above the city of Kirkenes.

German ships recorded an attack on the Jar Fjord convoy, but according to their reports, no damage was sustained. After dropping their bombs, the Kittyhawks, together with Airacobras, patrolled over Kirkenes and ensured that the Luftwaffe fighters were forced out of the strike area. From the combat flight log of 6th IAD: "At 1:15, to the south-east of the city of Kirkenes, at an altitude of 2,000m, three Kittyhawks conducted an unsuccessful air combat against two Bf 109s." Following the results of the air battles the Northern Fleet Air Force Headquarters credited one downed Bf 109 to the Guards Lieutenant M.E. Borzystiy, pilot of the 2nd GKAP.

Three groups of bombers of the 9th MTAD under the cover of fighters then began their attacks.

The first was a group of five Bostons of the 36th MTAP (leader – Captain P.I. Klyachugin) and 10 Airacobras of the 255th IAP (leader – Captain V.A. Burmatov). At 1:04, the Bostons dropped bombs on the north-eastern part of the city and port. According to pilots' observations, one bomb hit the north-eastern pier, another hit the transport ship, probably the *Florianopolis* (7,419grt). Anti-aircraft fire over the target hit one Airacobra which had to ditch in the sea. The pilot was rescued by torpedo boats. Luftwaffe fighters attempted to break through to the Bostons, but were unsuccessful, losing one FW 190 to Airacobra fire.

The second group consisted of five Bostons of the 36th MTAP (leader – Captain G.P. Khamkov) under the cover of eight Airacobras of the 255th IAP (leader – Captain F.E. Samarkov). At 1:05, the Bostons dropped bombs on the north-eastern and northern parts of the city. The crews reported the bombs hitting the 10,000-tonne transport. The bombs most likely hit the transport *Florianopolis* (7,419grt) again. Anti-aircraft fire hit the Boston of the group leader, and the aircraft crashed in the vicinity of the target.

One minute later, the third and final group of Bostons dropped their bomb load on the Kirkenes harbour facilities. The group consisted of five Bostons of the 9th GMTAP (leader – Guards Captain P.P. Gusev) covered by 10 Airacobras of the 2nd GKAP (leader – Guards Lieutenant P.D. Romanov). One Airacobra was shot down by anti-aircraft fire over the target; its pilot was killed.

The attack aircraft followed the Bostons. The group included six Il-2s (leader – Lieutenant M.M. Tamarov) and 10 Airacobras of the 20th IAP (leader – Captain E.V. Petrenko). At 1:07, the Il-2s dropped FAB-250 bombs from dive on the southern part of the city. According to the crews' observations, the attack resulted in several fires in the port and factory areas. On the way out of the strike, six Bf 109s attacked the group, but the fighters in cover, losing two Airacobras, managed to defend the Il-2s. One pilot of the Airacobras, Junior Lieutenant K.V. Timokhin, was killed, and the other, A.A. Chernukha, was taken prisoner. However, during the air battle Senior Lieutenant K.V. Boychenko and Lieutenant V.S. Shevchenko shot down one FW 190 each.

The last to appear over Kirkenes were three Pe-3s of the 95th IAP under the cover of eight Airacobras of the 20th IAP. Actually, they were supposed to appear first, even before the Kittyhawk fighter-bomber group, but in fact they arrived later than the other groups. The task of the group was the laying of mines in Beck Fjord. At 1:55, the heavy fighters dropped FAB-250 bombs without detonators in the target area. The Germans were unimpressed with this mine placement. Luftwaffe fighters attempted to attack the group, but the Airacobras of the 20th IAP repulsed the attack, shooting down two Luftwaffe fighters.

Following all the attack and distraction groups, the reconnaissance aircraft of the 118th RAP appeared over Kirkenes to record the damage. The main success was the destruction of the steamer *Florianopolis*, which had been damaged by attack aircraft on 17 June. Two or three bombs, according to various sources, hit the ship, destroying it. The 36th MTAP, that had recently joined the Northern Fleet Air Force, achieved its first success against enemy ships. The minesweepers M-31, M-202, M-252, and the submarine hunter UJ-1212 were lightly damaged by nearby bomb explosions. On 28 June, the Germans estimated the final damage. As a consequence of two Soviet air strikes, the losses to the German army and navy were tangible. The ore processing plant was seriously damaged by the strike. More than 20 warehouses with ammunition and military supplies of the German armed forces were destroyed or damaged. A dozen and a half office and accommodation buildings and barracks were damaged. The Viking Pier at the port was destroyed. The Soviet aircraft bombed rather accurately: the Norwegians only had four civilian houses burnt down. The casualties of the German forces included 11 dead, 39 badly wounded and 57 lightly wounded. The Norwegians had one casualty.

The German anti-aircraft defence urgently needed to save its face somehow, and it did. The Luftwaffe fighters of the III./JG 5, reported 56 (fifty-six!) victories. The Kirkenes anti-aircraft artillery claimed 18 victories, while the ship's gunners credited only three. The Northern Fleet Air Force pilots were credited with 12 victories, but German records show only two lost fighters. The first was Bf 109G-6, tactical number 'White 11', the pilot of which was *Unteroffizier* Hermann Kesseler of the 7./JG 5. German documents confirm his death in air combat. The second was a Luftwaffe fighter whose pilot was picked up by mountain huntsmen, while the aircraft itself set a small fire in the forest.

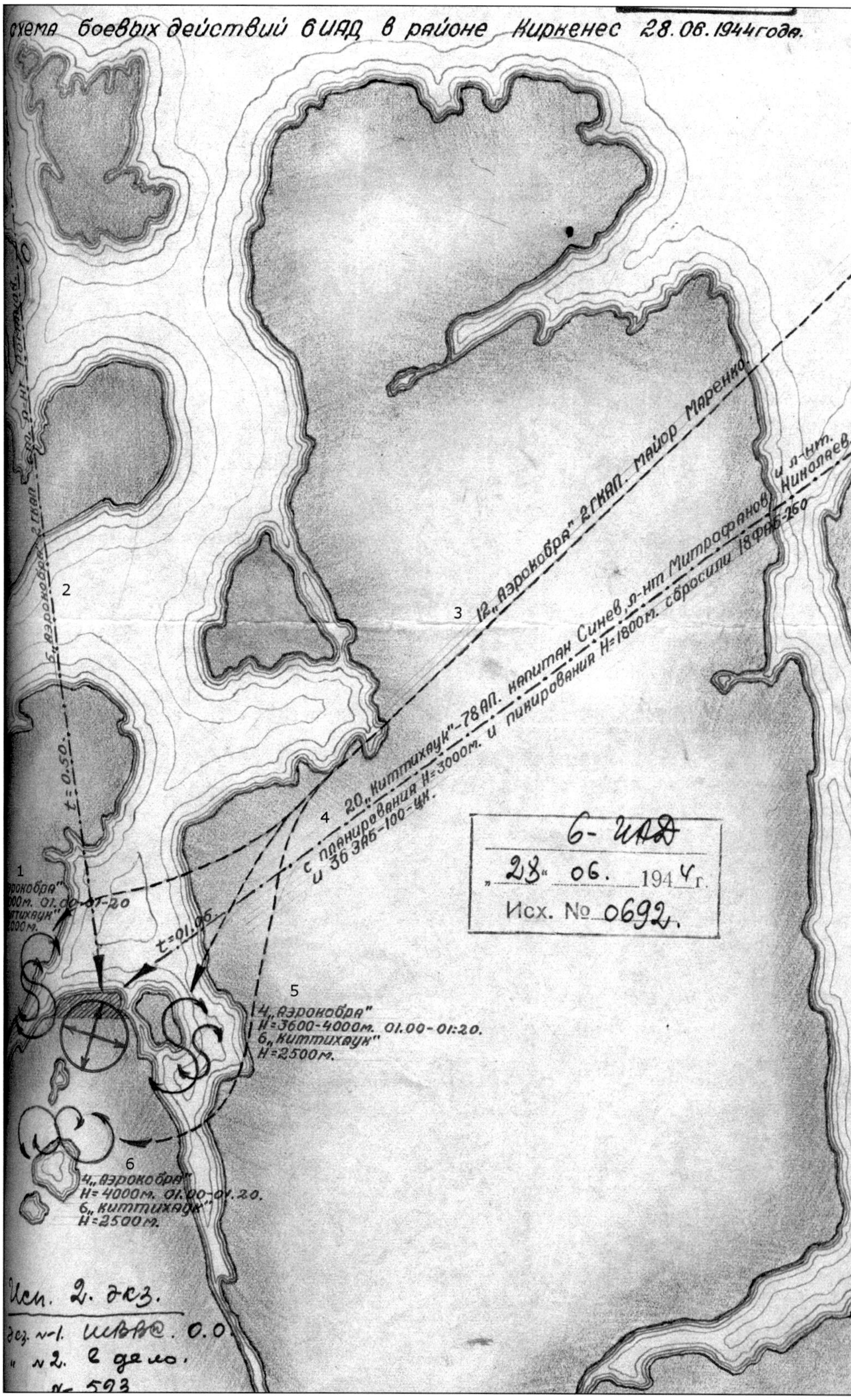

Plan of attack on Kirkenes by the aircraft of the 6th IAD, 28 June 1944.
1 – 1:00–1:20. Four Airacobras, altitude 4,000m. Six Kittyhawks, altitude 2,000m.
2 – 0:50. Five Airacobras of the 2nd GKAP, led by Senior Lieutenant Romanov.
3 – Twelve Airacobras of the 2nd GKAP, led by Major Marenko.
4 – 1:05. Twenty Kittyhawks of the 78th IAP, led by Captain Sinev, Lieutenant Mitrofanov and Lieutenant Nikolayev, dropped 18 FAB-250s and 36 ZAB-100TsK from horizontal flight at altitude of 3,000m and from dive from altitude of 1,800m.
5 – 1:00–1:20. Four Airacobras, altitude 3,600–4,000m. Six Kittyhawks, altitude 2,500m.
6 – 1:00–1:20. Four Airacobras, altitude 4,000m. Six Kittyhawks, altitude 2,500m.

2
KITTYHAWKS, JULY 1944

In July 1944 both fighter-bomber regiments carried out a large number of attacks against naval targets. Unfortunately, it became the last month in which the 27th IAP operated against enemy ships. The Kittyhawks were inferior to Airacobras in terms of their flying characteristics, but the regiments of the 6th IAD still had to carry out escorting of the torpedo bombers, bomber and attack aircraft.

As of 1 July 1944, the 27th IAP had 20 serviceable and six unserviceable Kittyhawks on its strength. In addition, the inventory of the regiment included one trainer Kittyhawk and one trainer Hurricane with dual controls, two unserviceable Hurricanes, one unserviceable Hurricane that served as a cargo aircraft, and one unserviceable U-2 trainer. All aircraft of the regiment but one unserviceable Hurricane were stationed at the Kildin airfield.

During the month, the 27th IAP carried out 134 combat flights, 51 of which were directed against ships and convoys. During the air battles, the regiment pilots shot down two Bf 109s. The losses during the month included two Kittyhawks and one Hurricane. Two pilots did not return from combat missions.

The second regiment of the 6th IAD which operated Kittyhawks, the 78th IAP, had 30 serviceable Kittyhawks and one serviceable trainer Kittyhawk with dual controls, as of 1 July 1944. All aircraft of the regiment were based at the Vaenga-2 airfield. However, on 18 July 1944, the regiment was transferred from the Vaenga-2 airfield to the Rosta airfield, from where it conducted combat flights until January 1945.

In July 1944, the 78th IAP carried out 148 combat flight, 63 of which were directed against ships and convoys, 34 bomb strikes against enemy bases and ports, and eight for bombing the enemy airfields. The regiment's pilots were credited with nine shot-down Bf 109s. The regiment lost seven Kittyhawks along with their pilots during combat missions.

The reconnaissance aircraft regiment also continued to operate Kittyhawks. As of 1 July 1944, the 118th RAP had 37 aircraft in service, including nine Kittyhawks.

4 July

It all started again with reconnaissance… A Yak-9 reconnaissance aircraft of the 118th RAP piloted by Lieutenant S.I. Pankrashin made several approaches to perform vertical and oblique photographing of Kirkenes. At 16:35, the pilot reported: south of Renö Island there were three transport ships and three warships, in Elvenes Fjord – six transport ships, in Lang Fjord – four transport ships and 18–20 escort ships.

The arrival of convoy Rp.123.Ki was no secret to the Northern Fleet Air Force command, and it was not attacked on the way due to the bad weather. But the weather improved, and at 16:25 the Chief of Staff of the Northern Fleet Air Force gave preliminary orders to prepare for an attack. Massive strikes by bomber and attack aircraft were supposed to cause maximum damage: burn the port and warehouses of the city and the port of Kirkenes, and destroy the transports and guard ships at the piers and at the anchorage. A total of nine groups were to take part in the attack.

As in the previous attacks on Kirkenes, the Kittyhawks were tasked with striking the central part of the city. The bombing targets included service buildings, barracks of German soldiers and officers. After dropping the bombs, Kittyhawks were to sweep away the enemy fighters from the target area for 10–15 more minutes.

All strike groups were to attack simultaneously, at 20:03–20:08.

At 17:30 the commanders of air divisions were summoned to the Northern Fleet Air Force command post. They were given orders to strike, targets were allocated and the interaction of units and formations in the forthcoming strike was determined. After receiving the orders, the groups prepared for the mission and set off to the target.

The first group dropped bombs on targets in Kirkenes at 20:03. The group consisted of the aircraft of the 78th IAP, led by Senior Lieutenant P.I. Sakharov and included eighteen Kittyhawk fighter-bombers and two Kittyhawks carrying photographic equipment to monitor the results of the strike. From the combat flight log of the 6th IAD:

> Bombs were dropped on the port of Kirkenes from horizontal flight at 2,000–1,800m, and from dives at an altitude of 1,000m. The pilots observed seven fires in the city. One transport of 3,500 tonnes displacement was sunk. The aircraft sustained heavy anti-aircraft fire over the target.

After developing and analysing the pictures of the results of the attack on Kirkenes, it was found out that the Kittyhawk bombs destroyed the electric substation and the fuel tanks located near it. This is also confirmed by German documents. After dropping their bombs, the Kittyhawks patrolled over Kirkenes in search of Luftwaffe fighters, and the latter were not long in coming. From the combat flight log of the 6th IAD:

> 20:10–20:15, Kirkenes area, the aircraft were engaged in an air combat against 10 Bf 109s at an altitude of 3,000–1,500m. As a result of the combat, Senior Lieutenant Boychenko shot down one Bf 109, which came down five to seven kilometres south-east of Kirkenes. Senior Lieutenant Sakharov shot down one Bf 109, falling north of Hego. Lieutenant Shvailakh shot down one Bf 109, which fell two to three kilometres south-east of Kirkenes. Junior Lieutenant Proyavko shot down one Bf 109, which fell near Kirkenes.

Based on the results of the air battle, the Northern Fleet Air Force Headquarters credited one downed Bf 109 each to the pilots of 78th IAP Senior Lieutenant P.I. Sakharov and Lieutenant A.Y. Shvailakh and pilot of 27th IAP Senior Lieutenant M.I. Boychenko. The Germans did not want to be 'whipping boys' and managed to damage three Kittyhawks piloted by Lieutenant A.F. Nikolayev, Junior Lieutenants D.P. Dzyuba and A.S. Volkov in the air battle. Despite the damage, the pilots were able to land at Pummanki airfield.

The second group consisting of five Bostons of the 36th MTAP (leader – Major P.N. Obukhov) and eight Airacobras of the 255th IAP (leader – Senior Lieutenant P.D. Bogdanov), and the third consisting of five Bostons of the 36th MTAP (leader – Captain I. Ilyushin) and eight Airacobras of 255th IAP (leader – Captain F. Samarkov) dropped bombs on the ore processing plant between 20:00–20:02. As a result of the strike, according to German documents, the plant was so severely damaged that it could not be restored in 1944. The crews observed three heavy explosions near the residential buildings, warehouses and port area, another bomb exploded near the railroad tracks. Four Bf 109s, which attacked both groups, succeeded in shooting down one Boston, the crew of which was killed. The escort Airacobras that joined the combat shot down three Bf 109s at the cost of one damaged Airacobra, whose pilot managed to bring his aircraft to Vaenga-1.

The fourth group, consisting of five Bostons of the 36th MTAP (leader – Major S.F. Pereverzin) and eight Airacobras of the 255th IAP, and the fifth group, consisting of five Bostons of the 36th MTAP (leader – Major M.M. Prokofyev) and eight Airacobras of the 2nd GKAP (leader – Guards Captain P.L. Kolomiets) dropped bombs at 20:09 on the port and transports moored to the pier. The crews observed three strong explosions in the port area. The nature of the explosions led them to conclude that a warehouse with liquid fuel and two ammunition depots had been hit. According to the pictures captured by reconnaissance aircraft, fires in the port continued throughout the day. After dropping the bombs, one Boston was shot down by anti-aircraft fire. The escort Airacobras fought against two groups of Luftwaffe Bf 109s of eight aircraft in total over the target area and during the withdrawal. As a result, the Soviet pilots were credited with one Bf 109 and one more was presumably shot down, but one Airacobra of the 2nd GKAP did not return from the combat mission and its pilot was killed.

The sixth group, consisting of five Bostons of the 9th GMTAP (leader – Guards Captain P.P. Gusev) and eight Airacobras of the 2nd GKAP (leader – Guards Captain S.M. Loginov), dropped their bombs at 20:04. According to the Northern Fleet Air Force Headquarters, the bombing was not aimed properly: the bombs fell in the hills and did not harm anyone. The group returned home safely.

The seventh group, consisting of Pe-3s of the 95th IAP under cover of Airacobras of the 20th IAP, did not participate in the strike for technical reasons.

The eighth group, consisting of six Il-2s (leader – Major G.V. Pavlov) under cover of 10 Airacobras of the 20th IAP (leader – Captain E.V. Petrenko), and the ninth group, consisting of five Il-2s (leader – Senior Lieutenant M.M. Tamarov), under cover of 10 Yaks of the 20th IAP (leader – Lieutenant Colonel D.A. Petrov), departed one after the other at 19:17. Having gathered over Vaenga-2 airfield, the groups flew to Kirkenes. Though the attack aircraft were 21 minutes late for take-off, they made the strike on time, at 20:08. The groups approached their target from the north-east and attacked transport ships that were anchored near Renö Island. All attack aircraft carried two FAB-250s each, but only the eighth group achieved relative success. At 20:08, led by the regiment commander, the group attacked the enemy transports in the Beck Fjord, two kilometres south of Renö Island. None of the bombs dropped from the attack aircraft hit the target, but the submarine hunters UJ-1212 and UJ-1222 were lightly damaged by the cannon and machine-+gun fire.

The ninth group, simultaneously with the eighth, attacked German ships and vessels in Beck Fjord from the eastern side of the island of Renö. According to the reports of the crews of the attack aircraft, the bombs were dropped unsuccessfully and did not hit the enemy ships.

Strikes by the Bostons and Kittyhawks caused serious damage to the city. Several Norwegian houses caught fire as a result of the bombing. Strong winds quickly fanned the fires, and about half the town was destroyed as a result. The list of losses included a destroyed switchboard station, fuel tanks and lots of coal. The ammunition bunker and the food supplies of the navy's communications service

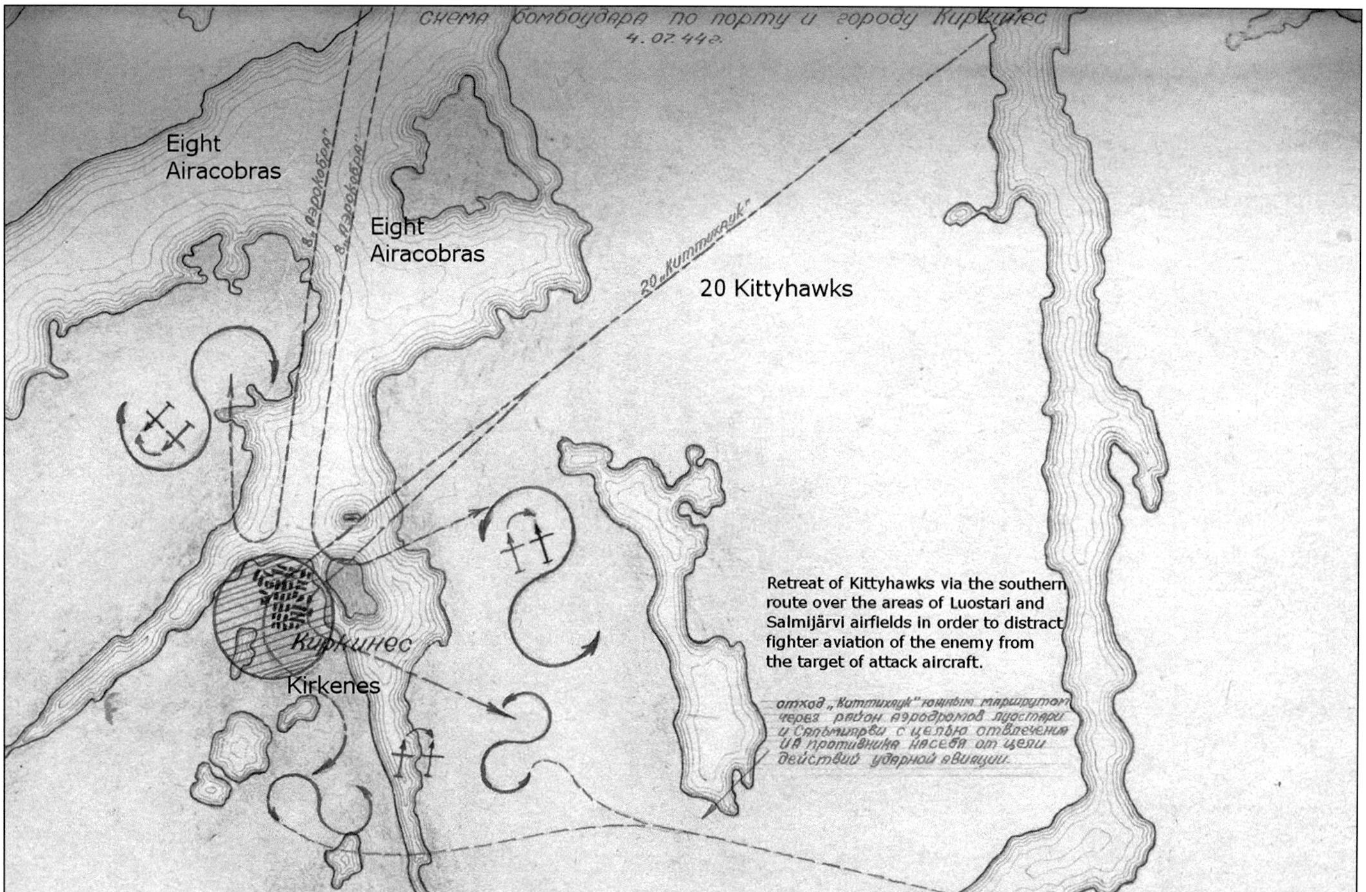

Plan of attack on Kirkenes by the aircraft of the 6th IAD, 4 July 1944.

Photo reconnaissance report of the results of the air strike on Kirkenes, 4 July 1944.

were also damaged. Three German soldiers were wounded. The port of Kirkenes and the ships in it were not damaged.

Luftwaffe fighters claimed 27 victories over Soviet aircraft, with two more victories credited by German anti-aircraft gunners. Actual losses of the Northern Fleet Air Force included two Boston and one Airacobra aircraft, of which one Boston was shot down by anti-aircraft fire. Based on the results of the strike, the Northern Fleet Air Force Headquarters credited seven downed Bf 109s to the pilots, while another Bf 109 was counted as a presumable victory. So far, the found German records show that three Bf 109s did not return from the combat mission. All of them were from 8./JG 5: the first was Bf 109G-6, W.Nr. 411091, tactical number 'Black 4', shot down over Kirkenes, the pilot, *Gefr.* Friedrich Elken, was killed. The second, Bf 109G-6, W.Nr. 412213, code letters 'RX+MW', crashed six kilometres west of Luostari airfield during an emergency landing. The pilot survived. The third, Bf 109F 4, W.Nr. 8636, tactical number 'Black 15', crashed while landing at Luostari airfield. The pilot survived.

5 July

At 8:24, four Kittyhawk fighter-bombers of 27th IAP (leader – Senior Lieutenant A.P. Anuchin) took off for a 'free hunting' mission in Varanger Fjord. At about 9:00, the pilots spotted a self-propelled barge near Skallnesset Cape. From the combat flight log of the 6th IAD:

> At 9:03, the aircraft, flying at low altitude, fired machine guns and carried out a skip-bombing attack from 25–30m altitude, at 100–150m distance, on an enemy self-propelled barge, 5–10km to the north of Eckerö. As a result of the strike, one self-propelled barge was damaged by two FAB-100s, which exploded at the distance of 15m.

The Northern Fleet Air Force Headquarters credited Lieutenant N.I. Dyogtev with the damage to the self-propelled barge. In fact, the vessel was the Norwegian motorboat *Hugin*, sailing without cargo, the crew of which lost one man killed and one wounded.

7 July

Despite the challenging weather conditions, the pilots of the 27th IAP flew three group 'free-hunting' missions against enemy ships in the Eckerö–Vardö–Hamningberg area.

During the first of these missions, a group of four Kittyhawk fighter-bombers of the 27th IAP (leader – Senior Lieutenant A.P. Anuchin) attacked the village of Skällelv as they had not spotted any enemy ships. At 17:06, the fighter-bombers dropped bombs on the village and, according to the pilots' report, Lieutenant N.I. Dyogtev sank two motorboats. The German records do not reflect this event, so it can be concluded that it was fishing boats that were hit.

Meanwhile, the second group of Kittyhawks found a more interesting target. The four Kittyhawks (leader – Senior Lieutenant I.S. Yedush) took off at 16:33 and located a transport ship of 800–1,000 tonnes displacement near Harbaken Cape. Three Kittyhawks dropped bombs on the transport from an altitude of 600–400m, and the fourth dropped bombs on the warehouse on the shore. From the report of Senior Lieutenant I.S. Yedush:

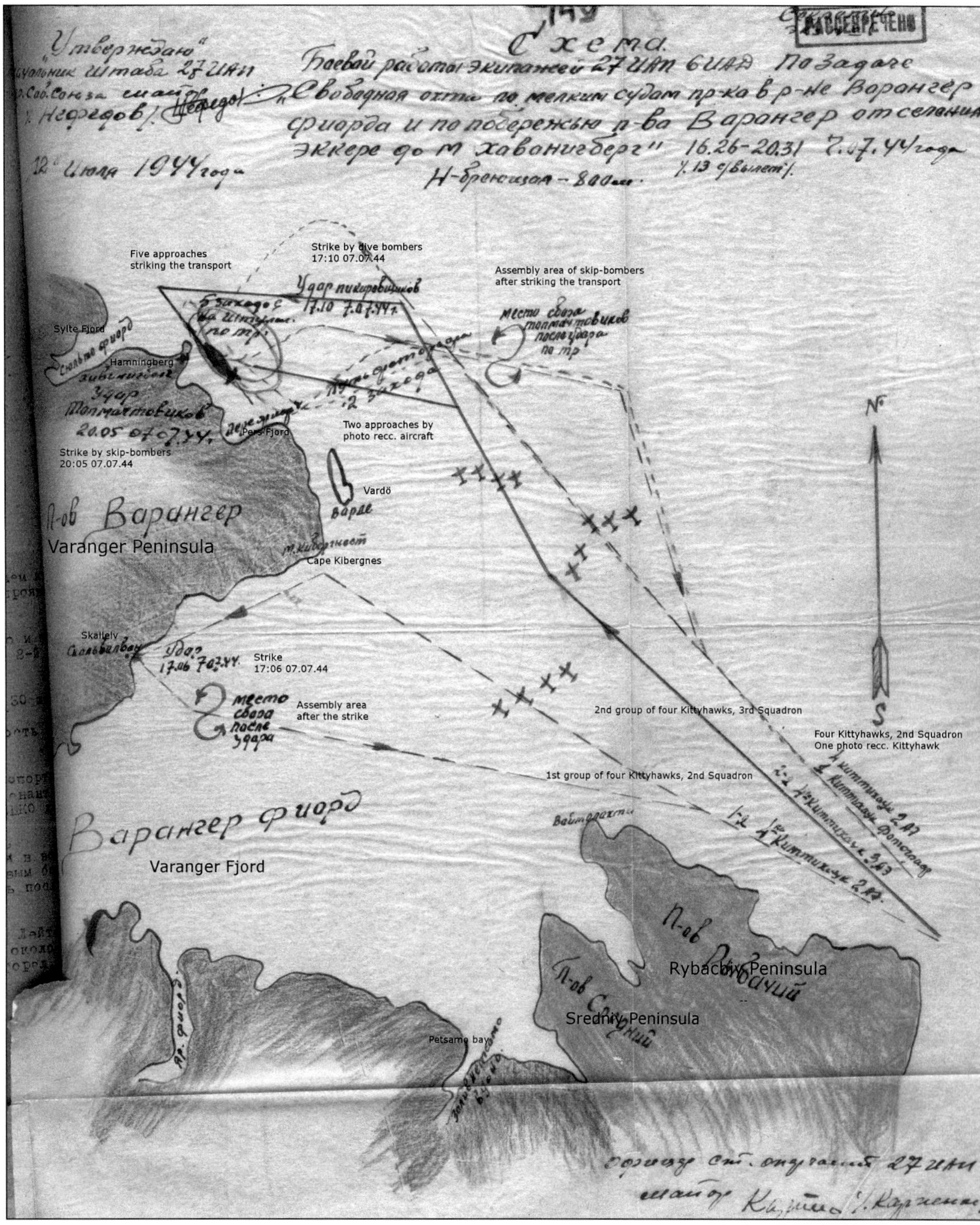

Plan of attack on the enemy ships by the 27th IAP Kittyhawks, 7 July 1944.

Lieutenant Bogdanov hit the stern of the transport with a direct hit from one FAB-100. The transport listed, shrouded in black smoke. We observed an explosion in the village of Havningsberg. After bombing the transport, I made six approaches on the transport, firing machine guns at it.

German documents describe this event as follows:

16:30 [Berlin time – Author's note], four enemy aircraft attacked the Norwegian boat *Ulløy* (T-53-F). The boat was set on fire. The Norwegian crew and passengers (32 people) were picked up by the Norwegian motorboat *Steinfjord*. As a result of the attack, 13 people are missing, along with six seriously and seven lightly wounded.

From the report of Lieutenant P.V. Bogdanov:

I attacked a transport of 800–1,000 tonnes displacement two kilometres off the shore of Havningsberg. The bomb exploded in the stern of the transport. After dropping bombs, I made five approaches with machine-gun fire. I fired mostly at 90 degrees to the transport. After each approach there was black smoke pouring from it. The transport had blue colouring with white stripes, the captain's cabin was located in the aft part of the transport.

The target of the attack, according to the pilots' observations, remained afloat, and the command of the 27th IAP believed that the Kittyhawks had only damaged the transport. In order to finish off the transport, a group of four Kittyhawks (leader – Senior Lieutenant B.G. Yermilin) took off. At 20:05, five to six kilometres to the south-east of Hamningberg, the group approaching from the south at 30m altitude bombed the transport from 200m distance using the skip-bombing method. The pilots thought they had finished off the transport, but they had not. The German documents describe this event as follows: "18:50 [Berlin time], three enemy aircraft dropped bombs on the boat that was still burning". Despite the miss of the skip-bombing group, the fate of the motorboat was sealed. On 8 July 1944, the burning wreck was towed to Vardö by motor ship *Edelgard* and at 6:00 sank in the inner breakwater.

9 July

The Kittyhawk pilots experienced unsuccessful missions as well successful ones. On the evening of 9 July, four Kittyhawks set off on a 'free hunting' mission along the Norwegian coast. From the report of Senior Lieutenant A.F. Nikolayev, leader of the four Kittyhawks of the 78th IAP:

> At 20:45 [the aircraft took off from the airfield – Author's note], the aircraft flew along the route Vaenga-2 – Set-Navolok – Tsyp-Navolok – Vardö – Berlevåg. At 22:00, we attacked a tugboat at Bos Fjord. Nothing was found on the communication lines up to Berlevåg, on the return route a tugboat was spotted in Bos Fjord and attacked by me. I observed a direct hit by one FAB-100. The tugboat sunk. The aircraft were subjected to anti-aircraft artillery fire near Berlevåg and at Beck Fjord.

German documents note "21:00-21:10 [Berlin time], Bos Fjord. Attack by four Il-2s on the motorboat *Ben Hur* chartered by Wehrmacht, 2.5km east of Holmen, in the Bos Fjord, with bombs and on-board armament". The Germans fired anti-aircraft guns from the shore batteries and the artillery barge AF-39. The motorboat was not damaged in any way. Following this attack the Kittyhawks spotted a German transport ship of 3,000 tonnes displacement. As they were already out of bombs, the only thing left to do was to transmit this information to the command of the 6th IAD. Fifteen minutes after the group of A.F. Nikolayev, at 21:00, four Kittyhawk fighter-bombers of the 78th IAP (leader – Lieutenant V. Kirichenko) took off. The mission was the same: 'free-hunting' for ships and vessels. Having failed to find any sea targets, at 21:50 the aircraft attacked the small port of Langbunes.

From the operations log book of the German 20th Army:

> At 21:42, about 10 P-40s carried out an attack on the field observation post five kilometres west from Kiberg, with bombs and onboard armament. Minor damage. Fighters [Luftwaffe – Author's note] being ferried to Svartnes flew past and shot down six Kittyhawks.

In fact, the Kittyhawks were attacked by eight Bf 109s of 8./JG 5. Based on the results of the air battle, the Northern Fleet Air Force Headquarters credited Lieutenant V.I. Kirichenko and Junior Lieutenant I.G. Kulikov with a downed Bf 109 each. The Germans acknowledge the loss of the Bf 109G-2, W.Nr. 14016, tactical number 'Black 2'. The pilot of the fighter, *Unteroffizier* Paul Freytag, was killed. Luftwaffe pilots credited six downed Soviet aircraft. In fact, two Kittyhawks did not return from the mission; their pilots, Junior Lieutenants I.G. Kulikov and D.N. Logvinov, were killed.

10 July

Operations on this day were a continuation of the previous day's missions. At 3:05, six Kittyhawks of the 27th IAP (leader – Senior Lieutenant A.P. Anuchin) took off to destroy a transport ship discovered on the evening of 9 July by A.F. Nikolayev's group. The fighter-bombers did not reach Bos Fjord due to deteriorating weather. After dropping bombs near Vardö, the aircraft turned home. The Germans registered with some surprise the flypast of six Il-2s over the sea to the east of Berlevåg – east of Vardö at 03:50. All Kittyhawks successfully reached the airfield and landed at 4:56.

In order to avoid a repeat of the previous day's air battles, the hunter Kittyhawks were escorted by eight Airacobras of the 2nd GKAP to cut off any Luftwaffe fighters. At 3:57, in the Peuravuono area, the Airacobras were engaged in air combat against three Bf 109s. Following the results of the air battle, the Northern Fleet Air Force Headquarters credited one Bf 109 to the Guards Lieutenant P.A. Kukhliyevskiy. German documents did not record this battle.

13 July

Reconnaissance aircraft of the 118th RAP spotted a small German convoy consisting of the transport *Reinhart L.M. Russ* and the patrol ships NKI-03 and NKI-05 on their way from Tana Fjord to Kirkenes. Ten Kittyhawk fighter-bombers of the 27th IAP (leader – Senior Lieutenant V.K. Vashchenko) under cover of eight Airacobras of the 2nd GKAP (leader – Guards Captain V.P. Maksimovich) took off to attack the convoy.

At 16:00, they struck the convoy near Sture Eckerö. Four Kittyhawks attacked by a skip-bombing method, and six aircraft bombed from a dive. The pairs of skip-bombers struck the patrol ships and the transports, but were unsuccessful. The dive bombers, on the other hand, achieved better results. Based on the reports of the pilots involved in the attack, it can be concluded that Lieutenant A.N. Nour succeeded in hitting the transports. According to his report: "I dropped the bombs from 600–400m altitude. I saw two of my bombs hit the transport with a displacement of 5,000–6,000 tonnes and they exploded between the middle and stern parts of the transport. The transport ship caught fire". From the report of German anti-aircraft gunners from steamer *Reinhart L.M. Russ*: "A bomb hit to the stern caused minor damage, the anti-aircraft commander was badly wounded by splinters. Consumption of ammunition: 160 pieces of 2cm shells, 218 rounds. Range 1,800–2000m". Luftwaffe fighters of the 7./JG 5 took off from Svartnes airfield, but were prudent enough not to engage Soviet aircraft.

Meanwhile, a reconnaissance aircraft of the 118th RAP spotted another target, a small transport ship, and transmitted the data to the Northern Fleet Air Force Headquarters. Six Kittyhawk fighter-bombers and two photo reconnaissance Kittyhawks of the 78th IAP (leader – Lieutenant V.I. Kirichenko) accompanied by six Airacobras of the 2nd GKAP took off to attack the transport.

At 18:36, Soviet aircraft attacked the Norwegian steamer *Floemann* (125grt) with a cargo of barracks and construction materials for Taarnet. Three skip-bombers and three dive bombers succeeded in hitting the ship. In the absence of German air cover, the Kittyhawks were joined by two Airacobras which struck the ship. Bombs and cannon and machine-gun fire caused a fire in the aft section of the ship. Among the crew and passengers, three were seriously wounded and three lightly. Two German motor minesweepers and the tug *Kure Fjord* tried to rescue the vessel, but all they managed to do was to ground it at the entrance to the Jar Fjord. Later , Norwegians tried to salvage the ship, but while being towed it was grounded where it was later destroyed. For unclear reasons, the pilots did not observe the result of the attack. The Northern Fleet Air Force Headquarters considered the attack unsuccessful.

The day ended with another attack by fighter-bombers against German ships. This time the target included two high-speed landing barges, which were discovered by a reconnaissance aircraft of the 118th RAP. Eleven Kittyhawk fighter-bombers and two photo reconnaissance Kittyhawks of the 27th IAP (leader – Senior Lieutenant A.P. Anuchin) flew under cover of 12 Airacobras of the 2nd GKAP (leader – Guards Captain P.L. Kolomiets). At 19:52, near Kobbholm Fjord, the Kittyhawks attacked the high-speed landing barges F-197 and F-226. The fighter-bombers dropped bombs from a dive but did not achieve a single direct hit on the barges. From the report of Senior Lieutenant I.S. Yedush:

> I attacked a barge in Kobbholm Fjord. Bombs exploded near the self-propelled barge and I used machine-gun fire to ignite it. I made four approaches to the self-propelled barge. Anuchin was the first to attack after which the barge caught fire. An anti-aircraft machine gun and a 37mm cannon were observed on the bow of the barge. The cannon was mounted in the bow of the barge and additional machine guns in the aft part. The barge was burning with black smoke which could be seen far away when flying from Pummanki.

As there were no Luftwaffe fighters, the escort Airacobras also joined the attack on the barges. From the report of the Guards Captain P.L. Kolomiets: "At 19:45, I attacked the self-propelled barge with cannon and machine-gun fire. The deck was hit". German sailors on the high-speed landing barges F-197 and F-226 experienced very unpleasant moments. According to a report of the mechanical engineer of the 7th Landing Ships Flotilla, the starboard engine of the F-226 was destroyed by a bomb explosion close to the board. On the F-197, machine-gun fire and splinters from bomb explosions created several small holes at waterline level, and three crew members were wounded. In addition to the barges, a Norwegian motorboat was presumably hit as well. From the report of Lieutenant N.I. Dyogtev, pilot of the Kittyhawk of the 27th IAP:

> I observed a bomb strike by the second group against the same target [high-speed landing barges – Author's note] without success and then their strike on the target with machine guns. No direct hits were observed. The bombs were exploding in close proximity. After firing on the barges with machine guns I saw one barge catch fire. I attacked a ship of 300–400 tonnes displacement, which was three to five kilometres behind the barges. I made four approaches together with one Airacobra, then the ship caught fire and headed for the shore.

The Northern Fleet Air Force Headquarters credited the pilot with the sinking of the passenger ship of 400 tonnes displacement. This time Luftwaffe fighters of the 8./JG 5 arrived in the battle area, although only by the time the bombing attack was over. The Germans claimed one victory, which is not confirmed by any records, and were attacked by Airacobras led by Guards Captain P.L. Kolomiets. From his report: "Departing from the target at an altitude of 1,000m north-west of Peuno I noticed three Bf 109s flying behind me at low altitude, which banked to the right towards the coast. Entering a dive, I caught up with the wingman and fired a long following burst from the distance of 200 to 400m at 0/4–1/4 target aspect ratio". A victory was credited to Guards Captain P.L. Kolomiets, but German documents say nothing about fighter losses on that day.

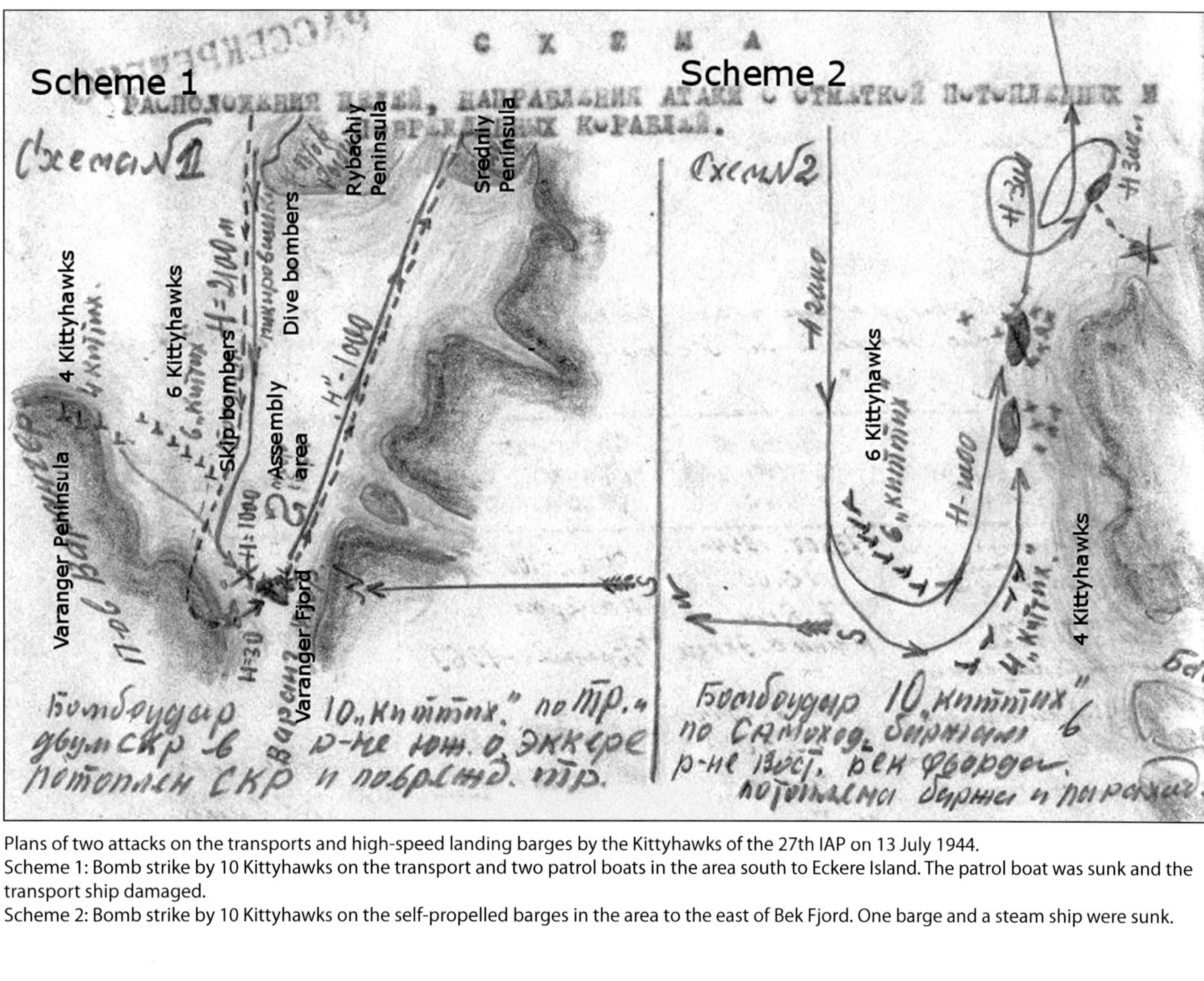

Plans of two attacks on the transports and high-speed landing barges by the Kittyhawks of the 27th IAP on 13 July 1944.
Scheme 1: Bomb strike by 10 Kittyhawks on the transport and two patrol boats in the area south to Eckere Island. The patrol boat was sunk and the transport ship damaged.
Scheme 2: Bomb strike by 10 Kittyhawks on the self-propelled barges in the area to the east of Bek Fjord. One barge and a steam ship were sunk.

Guards Captain P.L. Kolomiets, Hero of the Soviet Union.

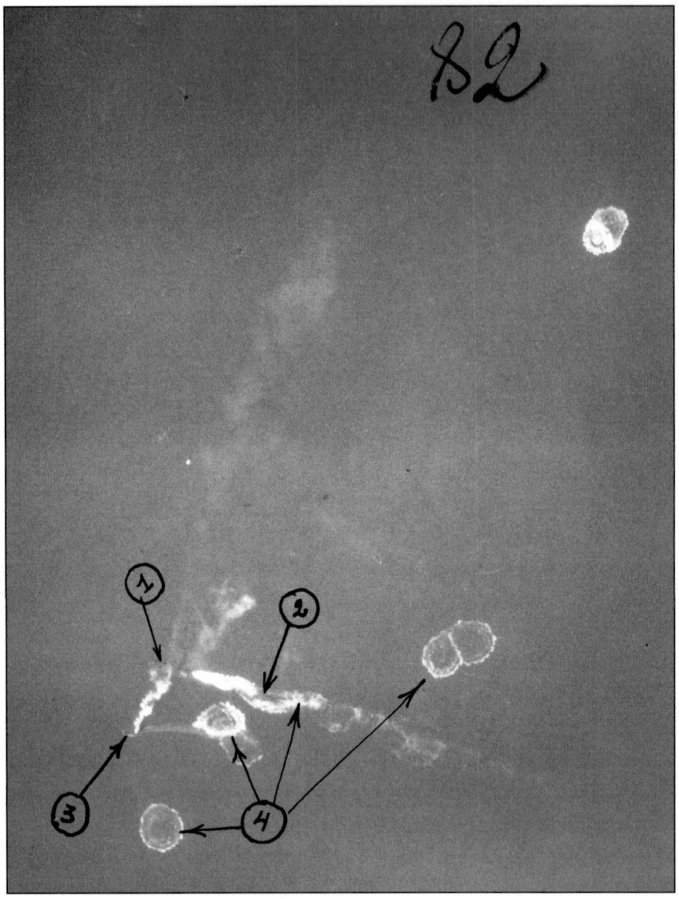

Photo reconnaissance report of the results of the air strike on the German convoy by Kittyhawks of the 27th IAP on 13 July 1944.

17 July

In the morning, the reconnaissance aircraft of the 118th RAP were able to take pictures of the German convoy Rp.124.Ki which arrived in Kirkenes on 16 July 1944. Due to bad weather, the convoy was not attacked by aircraft en route, and the Northern Fleet Air Force Headquarters decided to attack the ships and vessels of the convoy directly in Kirkenes. In addition to the ships and vessels, the Northern Fleet Air Force attacked the port and warehousing facilities.

The first attack was carried out by 16 Kittyhawk fighter-bombers and two photo-reconnaissance Kittyhawks of the 78th IAP (leader – Major V.I. Babernov) under the cover of eight Airacobras of the 2nd GKAP. The group took off at 18:50 and was over the target 40 minutes later. From the combat flight log of the 6th IAD:

> At 19:30, the aircraft dropped 16 FAB-250s from a horizontal flight at an altitude of 3,000m on the central part of the city, and 14 ZAB-100TsK and 18 FAB-100 bombs from a dive, from an altitude of 1,500m, on the Kirkenes power station. As a result of the strike, two bombs hit the power station, one hit the ore processing plant, two houses caught fire, two warehouses were burning.

As usual, after dropping the bombs, the Kittyhawks joined the Airacobras of the 2nd GKAP to 'sweep out' the Luftwaffe fighters. The latter were not long in coming. Several air combats took place over the city. From the combat flight log of the 6th IAD:

> At 19:35, near Kirkenes, at an altitude of 3,000m, four Kittyhawks conducted an air combat against six Bf 109s. As a result of the combat, Senior Lieutenant Batrakov shot down one Bf 109, which fell in the vicinity of Lake Rosyan-Yarvi (south-east of Kirkenes).

Based on the results of the air combats, the Northern Fleet Air Force Headquarters credited Guards Senior Lieutenant N.A. Bokiy, Guards Lieutenant V.I. Maslennikov, and Junior Lieutenant N.I. Zapalenov of the 2nd GKAP and Senior Lieutenant A.I. Batrakov of the 78th IAP with one downed Bf 109 each. Two more pilots of the 2nd GKAP, Guards Lieutenant N.M. Matveev and Junior Lieutenant M.E. Borzystiy credited one presumably downed Bf 109 each. However, in the course of the combat one Airacobra of the 2nd GKAP (piloted by Guards Junior Lieutenant S.A. Frolenkov) and one Kittyhawk of the 78th IAP (piloted by Lieutenant N.V. Vasilyev) were shot down. Both pilots were killed. The Kittyhawk flown by Senior Lieutenant A.I. Batrakov was hit by a Bf 109 and collided with it, so only his extensive flying experience and luck enabled the pilot to bring the aircraft back to his home airfield. He made an emergency landing, and the aircraft was repaired by the regiment's technicians.

The fighter-bombers were followed by three groups of Bostons of the 5th MTAD under the cover of Airacobras of the 255th IAP.

Five Bostons of the 36th MTAP (leader – Major M.M. Prokofyev) dropped bombs on the plant's pier and ore processing plant. Explosions and fires were observed as a result.

Five Bostons of the 36th MTAP (leader – Captain V.P. Rukovitsyn) dropped bombs on the ore processing plant and the southern part of the city. According to the observations of the crews, fires broke out in the places where the bombs had fallen.

Five Bostons of 36th MTAP (leader – Captain V.P. Novitskiy) dropped bombs on the northern pier and ore processing plant. The crews observed explosions and fires at the targets.

Luftwaffe fighters managed to break through to the Bostons, and they hit three aircraft over the city. All of the damaged bombers managed to reach Pummanki airfield, but two of them had to be written off. The gunners of the Bostons shot down two Luftwaffe fighters, but two gunners were killed and two others wounded. Airacobras of the 255th IAP, covering the Bostons, shot down three Luftwaffe fighters and lost one Airacobra. Its pilot, Junior Lieutenant S.M. Shulika, was killed. German documents assess the results of the Boston strike rather modestly. In Kirkenes, two barracks and one vehicle were damaged and four German servicemen were wounded. Only 10–12 bombs fell on the port where one motorboat was damaged. In addition, the steamships *Dockenhuden, Sevre* and *Hartmut* were lightly damaged by splinters and cannon and machine-gun fire.

The task for the attacking aircraft in the strike on Kirkenes on 17 July 1944 was to hit the transport ships near the Island of Renö. For this purpose, the 46th ShAP allocated 18 aircraft.

At 19:10, a group of six Il-2s (leader – Captain S.A. Gulyaev) took off from Vaenga-2 airfield under the cover of 10 Airacobras of the 20th IAP (leader – Captain A.K. Tarasov). At 19:20, they were followed by six Il-2s (leader – Senior Lieutenant M.M. Tamarov), covered by six Airacobras and two Yak-7Bs of the 20th IAP (leader – Lieutenant I.S. Mikhailov). However, by 19:55, both groups had already returned to the airfield due to bad weather conditions: Motovskiy Bay up to Kildin Island was covered by fog. Six more Il-2s (leader – Senior Lieutenant L.S. Uskrebkov), under cover of eight Yaks of the 20th IAP took off from Pummanki airfield. They did not encounter any fog on the way and were able to reach their target. At 20:16, six attack aircraft struck the transports south of the island of Renö.

The Luftwaffe fighters, who made 37 combat flights to intercept the Soviet aircraft over Kirkenes, did not hesitate to claim 39 victories this time. Three more victories were claimed by the German anti-aircraft batteries. Losses of the Northern Fleet Air Force from action of enemy fighters and anti-aircraft fire amounted to five aircraft. Based on the results of the air combats, the Northern Fleet Air Force Headquarters credited nine German fighters to the fighter pilots and gunners of the Bostons. The currently known losses of Luftwaffe fighters are one aircraft. It was Bf 109G-6, W.Nr. 411959, of the 7./JG 5; its pilot, *Unteroffizier* Werner Hinz, was killed.

21 July

At 0:45, a Kittyhawk reconnaissance aircraft of the 118th RAP spotted a large German convoy. This was convoy Ki.124.Lf leaving Kirkenes for the Lo Fjord. The convoy consisted of minesweepers M-31, M-35, M-154, M-251, M-252, patrol ships V-6101, V-6102, V-6107, V-6110, V-6111, V-6112, V-6115, submarine hunters UJ-1211, UJ-1212, UJ-1220, UJ-1222, motor minesweepers R-154, R-159, R-160, R-202, R-301, R-304, R-308, R-310, steamers *Santos* (5,943grt), *Poseidon* (3,911grt), *Dockenhuden* (3,525grt), *Ditmar Koel* (4,479grt), *Paloma* (932grt), *Hartmut* (2,713grt), *Leba* (1,586grt), tankers *Marsteinen* (765grt) and *Feiestein* (462grt). The convoy left Kirkenes on the evening of 20 July. The command of the Northern Fleet Air Force ordered the 6th IAD to conduct a series of strikes against the convoy.

The first to attack the convoy were eight fighter-bombers and two Kittyhawk photo reconnaissance aircraft of the 78th IAP (leader – Senior Lieutenant A.I. Batrakov) under the cover of eight Airacobras of the 2nd GKAP. At 3:03, near Kibergnes, they attacked the rear of the convoy using the skip-bombing method. From the report of Guards Captain S.M. Loginov, the 2nd GKAP: "The Kittyhawk of Senior Lieutenant Batrakov achieved a direct hit on the patrol ship. [This] Exploded". From the report of the commander of the motor minesweeper R-159:

> One of the Kittyhawks unexpectedly attacked from a low cloud, fired at the boat with 12.7mm machine guns and dropped two bombs. One of them fell 20m behind, in the wake, and the second exploded in close proximity to the port side. Another aircraft dropped one more bomb, which fell in front of the bow of the boat. The ship's port engine was disabled and the 3.7cm gun was damaged. Two of the engine crew members were lightly wounded.

In addition to the damaged R-159, minesweeper V-6101 was also hit by machine-gun fire. One crew member was lightly wounded. Due to the damage, the motor minesweeper R-159 was forced to leave the convoy and sail for repairs to the port.

During the strike on the convoy, the Soviet aircraft were attacked by Bf 109s of 7./JG 5. From the report of Guards Captain S.M. Loginov: "At 3:10, I attacked a Bf 109 four kilometres to the east of the convoy, at target aspect ratio of 2/4, from a distance of 150m; the enemy aircraft fell down burning four kilometres from the convoy". Based on the results of the air combat, the Northern Fleet Air Force Headquarters credited Guards Captain S.M. Loginov of the 2nd GKAP and Junior Lieutenant N.M. Tishchenko of the 78th IAP with one downed Bf 109 each. The Airacobra of the 2nd GKAP flown by Guards Lieutenant N.M. Matveev did not return from the mission. The Luftwaffe pilots claimed one downed Soviet aircraft, at the same time losing Bf 109G-6, W.Nr. 411971; its pilot, *Unteroffizier* Wilhelm Mollenhauer, was killed.

At 2:48, six Kittyhawk fighter-bombers of the 27th IAP (leader – Senior Lieutenant I.S. Yedush) under cover of eight Airacobras of the 2nd GKAP took off to attack the convoy. Due to bad weather conditions, the group did not find the convoy and had to return. However, this initial failure did not deter the pilots of the 27th IAP, and they took off again, despite the lack of escort fighters, which had no time to refuel. Alas, this time it was a mistake. At 5:35, the same six Kittyhawk fighter-bombers of the 27th IAP (leader – Senior Lieutenant I.S. Yedush) attacked convoy Ki.124.Lf at Makkaur Cape. Bf 109s of 8./JG 5 suddenly attacked them, forced them to drop their bombs into the sea and to engage in air combat. The Luftwaffe fighters shot down two Kittyhawks; their pilots, Lieutenant D.I. Chinarin and Junior Lieutenant N.M. Yemelyanov, were killed, but for some reason the Luftwaffe pilots claimed only one victory. Based on the results of the air combat, the Northern Fleet Air Force Headquarters credited Lieutenant I.S. Yedush with one downed FW 190 and Lieutenant I.I. Maslennikov with one downed Bf 109. According to the available German data, the enemy suffered no losses, but there is still an opinion that Bf 109G-6, W.Nr. 411971, was shot down in this battle.

Eight Kittyhawk fighter-bombers of the 78th IAP (leader – Senior Lieutenant A.F. Nikolayev) under cover of four Airacobras of the 2nd GKAP were the last to attack the convoy. At 6:00, near Sylte Fjord they dropped bombs on it. From the report of Lieutenant N.P. Proyavko, pilot of a Kittyhawk of the 78th IAP: "At 5:55, I attacked a submarine hunter boat on the traverse of Makkaur Cape. I observed a direct hit of an FAB-100 bomb [of my own – Author's note] on the submarine hunter boat, the latter sank immediately". According to the combat log of the Motor Minesweepers Flotilla, no bombs hit the German ships, but the R-308 was damaged by machine-gun fire. Three of its crew were wounded. One Kittyhawk was shot down by anti-aircraft fire from German ships. From the accident report on the loss of the aircraft: "The aircraft received a direct hit from an anti-aircraft shell over the target. The aircraft ditched in water 15km north-west of Vaitolahti. The aircraft and its pilot sank". The pilot, Junior Lieutenant N.R. Lisichkin, died. During the retreat, the pilots of Kittyhawks and Airacobras engaged in an air combat against the fighters of 9./JG 5 without claiming victories. The Germans were not so modest, scoring five kills to their pilots.

22 July

In the morning, reconnaissance aircraft of the 118th RAP spotted a German convoy in Varanger Fjord. According to the German documents a group of German ships, consisting of four high-speed landing barges and a motor minesweeper, were looking for Soviet reconnaissance teams along the coast. At 12:27, 10 Kittyhawk fighter-bombers of the 78th IAP (leader – Captain P.I. Sakharov) under cover of 12 Airacobras of the 2nd GKAP (leader – Guards Major I.M. Sukhomlin) took off to strike the convoy in the area of Kibergnes. One Kittyhawk developed engine problems and turned home. Due to the bad weather conditions, the other aircraft did not reach the target and attacked a transport ship in Jar Fjord at 13:10. The attack could not be carried out using the skip-bombing method, so the pilots carried out bombing from a horizontal flight, from an altitude of 40–50m. From the report of Captain P.I. Sakharov: "In

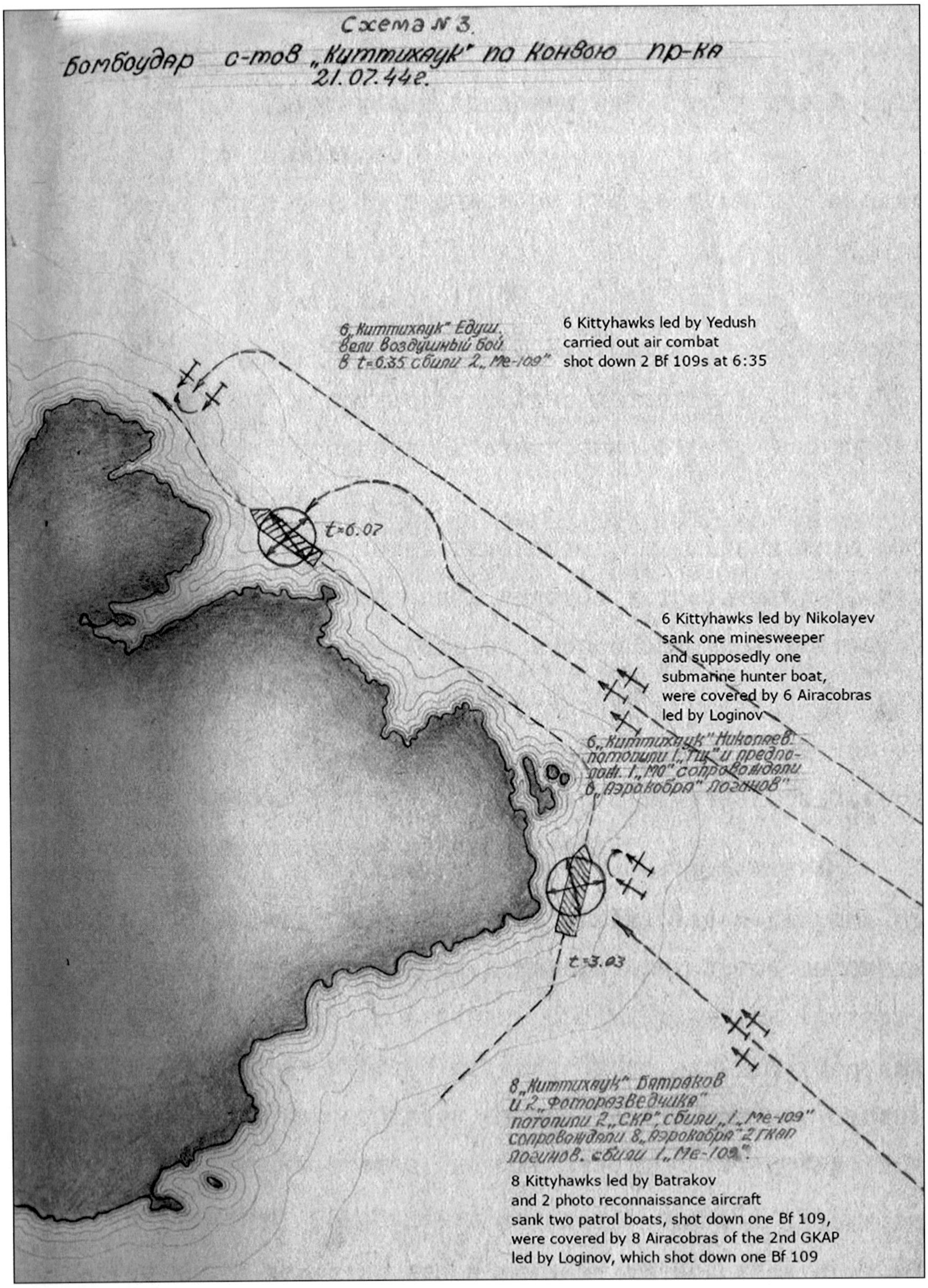

Plan of attack on the German convoy by the aircraft the 6th IAD on 21 July 1944.

Jar Fjord we attacked a transport of 1,500 tonnes displacement. The bombs fell with undershoot and overshoot. There were no hits in the target. We also fired machine guns at the transport. After that, it started emitting smoke from the stern, tilted and moored to the shore". The Dutch motor ship *Roerdomp* (280grt) was hit by fighter-bombers. The ship was damaged by machine-gun fire and ran aground. One crew member was wounded.

When the Kittyhawks came out of the strike, they were attacked by Bf 109s of the *Stab* III./JG 5 and 10. *Staffel* of the JG 5. In the course of the first attack, Luftwaffe fighters shot down two Kittyhawks piloted by Junior Lieutenants N.M. Tishchenko and A.S. Volkov. Both pilots were killed… Luftwaffe pilots claimed 13 victories without any losses of their own. It should be noted that *Fahnenjunker-Oberfeldwebel* Walter Schuck claimed seven (!!!) victories over Soviet aircraft in this combat. When the Airacobras entered the combat, Luftwaffe fighters began to withdraw. In the area of Rybachiy Peninsula, the enemy repeatedly attacked a group of Soviet aircraft. The Germans received reinforcements from 8./JG 5, whose pilots also claimed four victories without their losses. In fact, one Kittyhawk, piloted by Junior Lieutenant N.A. Nerubenko, was damaged. Despite his injury, the pilot managed to bring his aircraft back to the airfield. Basing on the results of the air combat, the Northern Fleet Air Force Headquarters credited the pilots of the 2nd GKAP, Guards Captain P.L. Kolomiets and Lieutenant E.I. Gredyushko with one downed Bf 109 each. In the 78th IAP, Captain P.I. Sakharov and Junior Lieutenant V.S. Bozhko credited one downed Bf 109 each.

Kittyhawk of the 78th IAP at the airfield.

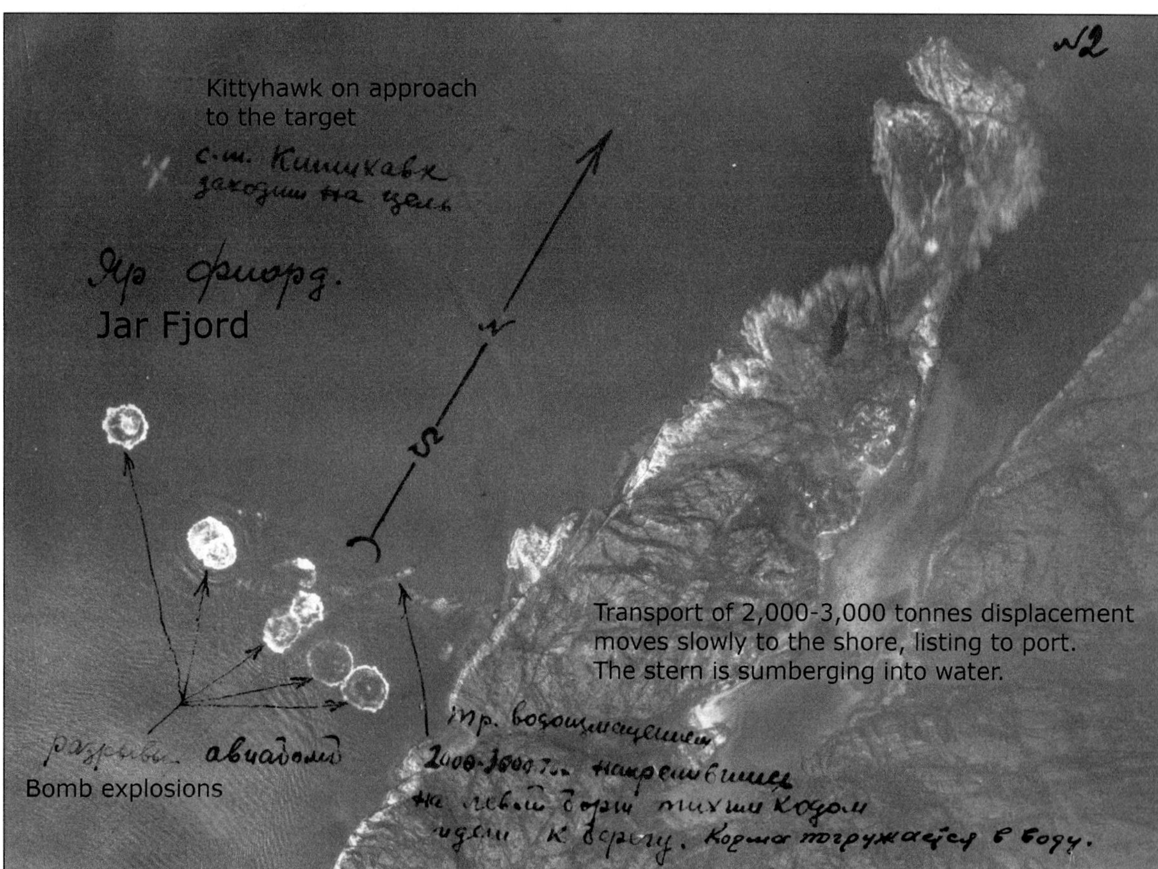

Kittyhawks of the 78th IAP attacking the Dutch motor ship *Roerdomp* on 22 July 1944.

28 July

On this day, the Soviet Air Force launched its third massive strike against Kirkenes in a month. According to the plan, eight Kittyhawk fighter-bombers of the 78th IAP under the cover of 12 Airacobras of the 2nd GKAP were to bomb the Luostari airfield and then block it together with the Airacobras. Bostons of the 5th MTAD were to attack the depots and ore processing plant in Kirkenes. Attack aircraft and Pe-3 heavy fighters of the 14th SAD were to target ships and boats moored in Kirkenes. The plans of the Northern Fleet Air Force command were conveyed to the flight crews and the operation commenced.

The first strike, as planned, was carried out against Luostari airfield by Kittyhawk fighter-bombers under the cover of Airacobras. The Kittyhawks took off at 13:05, but not all of them reached their target: the aircraft of Senior Lieutenant A.F. Nikolayev had to return due to engine trouble. The others hit the target at 13:34. From the combat flight log of 6th IAD: "At 13:34, 12 FAB-100s were dropped from a dive, from 1,700m altitude, on Luostari airfield. Four bomb explosions were observed at the eastern part of the airifield, two explosions in the eastern aircraft parking areas and four explosions at the northern part of the airfield". German documents indicate that a bomb hit on the airfield blew up a tent with six boxes of hand grenades stored in it. Anti-aircraft fire was fatal for one Kittyhawk. From the accident report on the loss of the aircraft: "While approaching the target, the aircraft were subjected to anti-aircraft artillery fire. The aircraft flown by Lieutenant Proyavko was hit, the pilot tried to bring it back home. 8–10km off the island of Heinya-Saari, it ditched in the water. The aircraft sank with the pilot". The pilot, Lieutenant N.P. Proyavko, died.

Luftwaffe fighters soon appeared and engaged in air combat over the airfield. From the combat flight log of the 6th IAD: "At 13:44, at 1,500-3,000m altitude, an air battle was fought against individual aircraft and groups of Bf 109 pairs. As a result of the combat, Lieutenant Kirichenko damaged a Bf 109". The Kittyhawk piloted by Captain D.I. Sinev was damaged in the air combat, left it and landed at its home airfield. Based on the results of the air combat, the Northern Fleet Air Force Headquarters credited one downed Bf 109 to the pilots of the 2nd GKAP, Guards Lieutenant P.L. Kolomiets, Guards Lieutenant E.I. Gredyushko and Guards Lieutenant N.A. Pilyus each. Lieutenant V.I. Kirichenko of the 78th IAP credited one damaged Bf 109.

The bombers of the 5th MTAD did not reach Kirkenes. Due to bad weather and low cloud cover, 16 Boston escorted by 26 Airacobras of the 255th IAP dropped 30 FAB-500s on an alternate target, Titovka. German documents confirm insignificant losses of equipment and damaged facilities.

However, the attack aircraft and Pe-3s of the 14th SAD were not prevented by the weather from attacking the targets in Kirkenes. At 14:05, 12 Il-2s of the 46th ShAP (leader – Captain S.A. Gulyaev) covered by 10 Airacobras of the 20th IAP and eight Kittyhawks of the 78th IAP attacked the enemy transport ships near Jakobsnes. A minute later, at 14:06, eight Pe-3s of the 95th IAP under cover of the eight Airacobras of the 20th IAP dropped bombs on the transports and the port of Kirkenes. According to German documents, the Soviet aircraft achieved a direct hit on the main pier, destroying it for 60m. German engineers and Soviet POWs repaired it for a fortnight. Two bombs fell on the South Varanger plant, several bombs hit the railway track and piles of coal. Three port warehouses were damaged by the explosions. There was minor damage to several smaller vessels: the steering gear was damaged on the tug *Kure Fjord*: a fire was started on the delivery vessel *Alta*, but it was extinguished. The crew of the tug *Ostland* had one sailor injured by machine-gun and cannon fire.

At 14:09, six Il-2s of the 46th ShAP (leader – Senior Lieutenant V.M. Skopintsev) under cover of eight Yak-9s of the 20th IAP dropped bombs from a dive on the transports to the south of Renö. The Soviet attack aircraft struck the transport ships *Dessau* and *Finse*, but missed. Four sailors on the *Dessau* were wounded by cannon and machine-gun fire. One attack aircraft was shot down by anti-aircraft fire, its crew died. The fighters of the 20th IAP were able to protect the Il-2s from enemy fighters on their way out of the attack and shot down two aircraft without any losses on their part.

The Luftwaffe fighters, having made 34 combat flights, claimed 12 downed Soviet aircraft, one more was claimed by the ship's anti-aircraft gunners. The Northern Fleet Air Force lost two aircraft, both to anti-aircraft artillery fire. Soviet pilots claimed five victories over Luftwaffe fighters. According to currently available information, the Germans lost one aircraft, a Bf 109G-2, W.Nr. 10565, tactical number 'Black 3', of the 8./JG 5. The pilot, *Unteroffizier* Stefan Mayer, was killed.

3
KITTYHAWKS, AUGUST & SEPTEMBER 1944

Due to bad weather in August 1944, the fighter-bombers of the 78th IAP flew just a few combat missions to hit enemy ships at sea. However, this does not mean that the Kittyhawks were inactive. They attacked ground targets in Kirkenes and blocked Luostari airfield together with the Airacobras of the 2nd GKAP, allowing the bombers and attack aircraft to strike ships and ground targets without being attacked by the enemy.

The main forces of the 78th IAP were based at the Rosta airfield, but on 9 August 1944 the 3rd Squadron of the regiment was redeployed to the Pummanki airfield, from where it attacked the German ground forces and ships on the enemy's communication lines.

In August 1944, the 78th IAP carried out 132 combat flights, of which only four were directed against ships and convoys. However, while the regiment did not operate against ships, it made 24 combat sorties against airfields, and 22 more against enemy artillery batteries. The Northern Fleet Air Force Headquarters credited three downed Bf 109s and one presumably downed Bf 109 to the regiment pilots. The regiment lost one Kittyhawk to anti-aircraft fire and two in the air combat, but no pilots were lost.

During August 1944, the 27th IAP fully converted to Airacobra fighters and thereafter only escorted the strike groups, without attacking ground or sea targets.

17 August

On the evening of 16 August 1944, between 20:42 and 22:00, a reconnaissance aircraft of the 118th RAP spotted nine transports and 10 escort ships in Kirkenes; the next day another reconnaissance aircraft managed to photograph them. After receiving data from the reconnaissance aircraft, the command of the Northern Fleet Air Force began to work out a plan of attack. As in previous strikes on Kirkenes, the Northern Fleet Air Force decided to attack the town, the port and the ore processing plant in addition to the ships. To suppress the activity of the enemy fighters based at Luostari, the command of the Northern Fleet Air Force allocated groups of 16 Airacobras of the 2nd GKAP and eight Kittyhawk fighter-bombers of the 78th IAP to block this airfield. The Kittyhawks were to carry out a bombing raid on the target and then take part in the blockade. Both groups were to arrive over Luostari 40 minutes before the strike on Kirkenes and patrol over the airfield for about an hour. Another group of eight Kittyhawks covered the bombers of the 9th GMTAP when they struck Kirkenes. One more group of six Kittyhawk fighter-bombers of the 78th IAP attacked the coastal batteries near Liinahamari because the guns were interfering with the landing of Soviet aircraft at the Pummanki airfield. Lastly, there was the rescue group for the pilots who may have to ditch their aircraft due to combat damage or failures. It consisted of a Catalina seaplane of the 118th RAP, covered by six Airacobras and four Kittyhawks. The seaplane was supposed to pick up pilots after forced landings in Varanger Fjord and Motovskiy Bay. The time of the Kirkenes attack was set at 11:00.

The first to strike, as planned, was the group performing the Luostari airfield blockade. After taking off from the Rosta airfield, eight Kittyhawk fighter-bombers of the 78th IAP (leader – Captain V.P. Strelnikov) set course for the Ura-Guba airfield to meet the Airacobra group. At 10:12, 15 Airacobras of the 2nd GKAP (leader – Guards Lieutenant Colonel D.F. Marenko), having detected the approach of the Kittyhawks, took off, joined them climbing, and went along the route Ura-Guba – Kuyrk Javr Lake– Luostari. At 10:14, one Airacobra, piloted by Guards Lieutenant N.G. Golodnikov, made an emergency landing due to mechanical failure. Fourteen Airacobras and eight Kittyhawks reached the target. At the moment the Kittyhawk aircraft began to dive, the right-hand group of seven Airacobras (leader – Guards Lieutenant Colonel D.F. Marenko) flew around the airfield from the north-west and, monitoring the air, headed for the area where the Kittyhawks were supposed to leave the bombing attack. The left-hand group of seven Airacobras circled the airfield from the south-west, covering the Kittyhawks during the bombing and when they came out of their dive. At 10:25, eight Kittyhawks successfully evaded heavy anti-aircraft fire and dropped 16 FAB-100s on Luostari airfield from 3,000-2,000m altitude without any resistance from enemy fighters. The pilots saw the bombs explode on the airfield and in the area where the aircraft were parked in the south-west of the airfield. After the strike, the Kittyhawks proceeded to the assembly area for further blockade of the airfield together with the Airacobras. The Airacobra pilots began searching for enemy fighters before approaching the target. No enemy aircraft were observed in the air at this time. Lieutenant Colonel D.F. Marenko, commander of the group, radioed the signal: "Fly to the planned assembly area".

When approaching the target, the pilots spotted a group of Bf 109s gaining altitude and other Bf 109s taking off from the Luostari airfield. A series of air combats against Bf 109s of the 9., 10. and 11. *Staffeln* of the JG 5 followed after which the Northern Fleet Air Force Headquarters credited one downed Bf 109 each to the pilots of the 2nd GKAP: Guards Lieutenant Colonel D.F. Marenko, Guards Captain V.P. Maksimovich, Guards Captain N.M. Didenko, Guards Senior Lieutenant V.I. Mukhin, Guards Lieutenant E.I. Gredyushko, Guards Junior Lieutenant P.A. Kukhliyevskiy. Luftwaffe fighters shot down two Airacobras, the pilots of which, Guards Lieutenant A.V. Zapodnikov and Guards Junior Lieutenant B.V. Kalinkin died.

The group of Kittyhawks was above the airfield at an altitude of 1,800–2,000m. In the heat of the battle, the aircraft formed a defensive circle and repelled individual attacks from enemy fighters. When four Bf 109s were trying to attack the Kittyhawks, Lieutenant A.S. Pavlov shot down one Bf 109, firing from above from a distance of 80–40m; the remaining Bf 109s escaped into the area patrolled by the Airacobras. It was the only victory which the Northern Fleet Air Force Headquarters credited to a Kittyhawk pilot in this battle.

The German anti-aircraft gunners managed to shoot down one Kittyhawk. From the accident report on the loss of the aircraft: "Junior Lieutenant Baev, while patrolling in the area, broke away from the formation and exposed himself to enemy anti-aircraft fire. The aircraft was damaged, the pilot made a forced landing on the enemy's territory and returned to the location of his troops three days later".

When the mission time was over, the group leader ordered the entire group to withdraw to the assembly area and to return to their home airfield. The Airacobras, having taken their place in combat order, covered the Kittyhawks on the route to the Ura-Guba airfield. Meanwhile, the strike groups approached Kirkenes and attacked the military facilities.

The group of bombers headed by Guards Captain P.P. Gusev was the first to attack the Germans. It consisted of five Bostons of the 9th GMTAP and eight Airacobras of the 255th IAP (leader – Captain F.E. Samarkov). At 10:58, the group dropped bombs on the approach to the target near the eastern moorings without causing any damage to the enemy, according to the information collected by the Fleet Air Force command. The group might have failed to aim properly after it was suddenly attacked by Luftwaffe Bf 109s. The enemy hit one Boston, which force-landed near Heinesaari. The Catalina flying boat arrived to rescue the floating crew, but was unable to bring anyone aboard. The crew was eventually rescued in the usual way, by a torpedo boat arriving from Sredniy Peninsula. Thus, the first attempt in the Northern Fleet to rescue crews by flying boat was a failure.

The second attack on Kirkenes was carried out almost simultaneously by two groups of Bostons. The first group consisted of five Bostons of the 36th MTAP (leader – Captain V.P. Novitskiy) and eight Airacobras of the 255th IAP (leader – Major A.E. Tulskiy); the second group consisted of five Bostons of the 36th MTAP (leader – Captain P.N. Obukhov) and eight Airacobras of the 255th IAP (leader – Senior Lieutenant A.F. Vlasov). At 10:58–11:00, both groups dropped bombs on the area of the north-western pier of the port of Kirkenes. The crews observed explosions in the northern part of the ore processing plant and in the area of the factory pier. The pilots of the groups reported the bombs hitting the ships and motorboats, but German documents do not confirm this. The fighters had no trouble repelling attempts by individual Bf 109s to attack the bombers, and the group went home. On the way back, it turned out that Captain P.N. Obukhov's Boston was seriously damaged by anti-aircraft fire, but the pilot managed to land the aircraft at Pummanki airfield. After landing, the aircraft was found to be seriously damaged and had to be written off.

The third attack on Kirkenes was carried out by a group of five Bostons of the 36th MTAP (leader – Major M.M. Prokofyev) and eight Airacobras of the 255th IAP (leader – Senior Lieutenant V.D. Artamonov). At 10:59, the bombers struck the north-eastern part of the city. The bombing caused two explosions followed by fire. Anti-aircraft artillery shot down one Boston, the crew of which was killed. There were no encounters with enemy fighters.

The fourth strike was conducted by a group consisting of five Il-4s of the 9th GMTAP (leader – Guards Captain K.F. Shkaruba) and eight Kittyhawk fighters of the 78th IAP (leader – Senior Lieutenant A.I. Batrakov). Six Yak-7s of the 20th IAP (leader – Senior Lieutenant I.P. Kuzhanov) were to have joined them, but in fact the Yaks joined one of the Boston groups and did not take part in the attack by this group. At 11:00, the bombers attacked the port moorings. The strike blew up one warehouse in the settlement of Jakobsnes and caused an explosion in a warehouse near the north-western pier. The attacking bombers, according to their crews' reports, were exposed to a barrage of anti-aircraft fire. Two Il-4s fell victim to it and were lost as well as their crews. The Kittyhawks of the 78th IAP which were covering the Il-4s managed to prevent the Luftwaffe fighters from breaking through to the bombers, but lost two Kittyhawks to anti-aircraft fire. The following was recorded in the report on the loss of the Kittyhawk of the 78th IAP piloted by Junior Lieutenant V.I. Volkov: "Flying in close proximity to Il-4s, the aircraft engine was damaged by heavy anti-aircraft fire. On the return route, near Tsyp-Navolok, the engine failed completely, the pilot belly-landed the aircraft". As a result, the aircraft was wrecked, the pilot was unharmed. Regarding the second Kittyhawk of the 78th IAP, piloted by Junior Lieutenant A.I. Strelnikov: "Flying in close proximity to Il-4s, the aircraft was damaged by heavy anti-aircraft fire [further text is illegible – Author's note]. On the return route, near the mouth of the Ura-Guba, the aircraft ran out of fuel and the engine stopped. The pilot belly-landed the aircraft in the hills." The aircraft was wrecked and the pilot slightly injured.

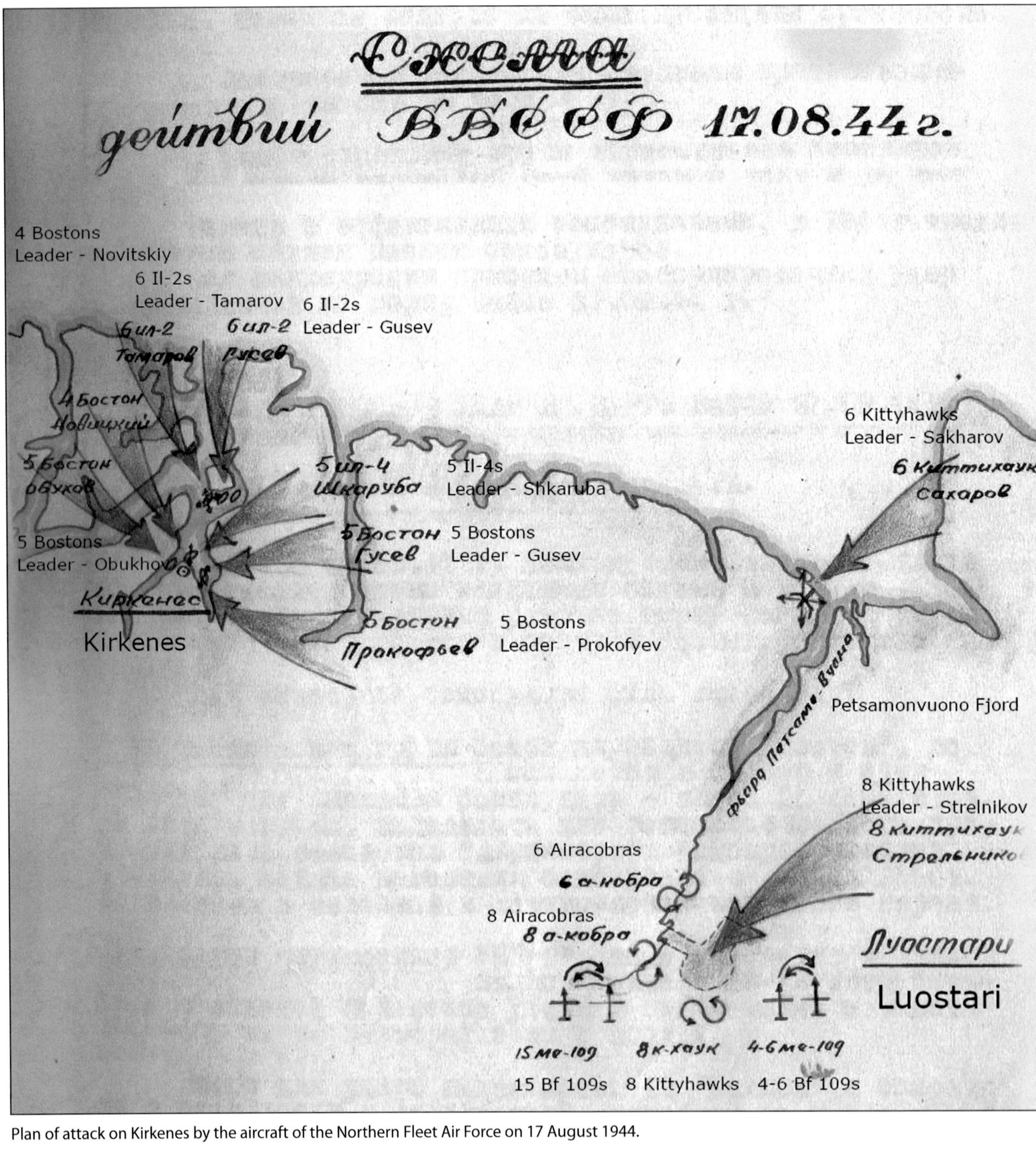

Plan of attack on Kirkenes by the aircraft of the Northern Fleet Air Force on 17 August 1944.

Perhaps the greatest success was achieved by two groups of attack aircraft of the 46th ShAP.

The first group consisted of six Il-2s (leader – Senior Lieutenant M.M. Tamarov) under cover of four Airacobras and four Yaks of the 20th IAP (leader – Captain E.V. Petrenko); the second group consisted of six Il-2s (leader – Senior Lieutenant E.M. Gusev) under cover of four Airacobras and four Yaks of the 20th IAP. At 11:00, two groups of attack aircraft struck the ships to the south of Renö Island. The first was the group of six aircraft led by Senior Lieutenant E.M. Gusev which bombed from a dive, followed group of six skip-bombers led by Senior Lieutenant M.M. Tamarov. According to the pilots' reports, they bombed three transport ships stationed south of the island of Renö. According to the German documents, the transports *Peter Bornhofen* (1,349grt) and *Sebu* (1,894grt) were attacked as well as the patrol ship V-6114 that was anchored next to them. The explosions caused *Peter Bornhofen* to sink, while the *Sebu* was damaged and grounded. In addition to the steamships, the artillery barge AF-28 was hit by a bomb, but its damage was repaired by nightfall. One sailor was lightly wounded by cannon and machine-gun fire on the artillery barge AF-39. Luftwaffe fighters attempted to prevent the attack, but were repulsed; Captain E.V. Petrenko shot down one Bf 109.

Summing up the results of this strike on Kirkenes, apart from the very effective actions by the attack aircraft, a conclusion can be made that the results were rather average. The strikes by Bostons on the city itself resulted in little effect. A heavy bomb destroyed about 50m of a 'gasoline pier', and one barrel of gasoline exploded on it. Eight German servicemen were injured.

German command reported greater success in repelling the attack. The aircraft of III./JG 5 took off to intercept Soviet aircraft. Luftwaffe fighters flew 34 combat missions, claiming 35 Soviet aircraft, and anti-aircraft gunners added nine more. The actual losses of the Soviet aircraft totalled nine. Judging by the crews' reports, the Kirkenes anti-aircraft artillery fire was well organised and murderous, resulting in the loss of four bombers. The loss of one bomber from a Luftwaffe fighter attack was considered by the command of the 5th MTAD as almost an exception to the rule, leading to the punishment of the fighter pilots of the 255th IAP who accompanied the downed bomber. The Soviet pilots claimed eight victories. Known losses of the Luftwaffe fighters were two aircraft: Bf 109G-6, W.Nr. 412228, tactical number 'Yellow 2', pilot, *Gefreiter* Günther Wien of the 9./JG 5 went missing in action near Petsamo; Bf 109G-6, W.Nr. 412320, tactical number 'White 6', pilot, *Leutnant* Karl-Heinz Schneider, of the 10./JG 5, crashed seven kilometres north-west of Petsamo airfield. The pilot was killed.

23 August

The Northern Fleet command decided to conduct a series of operations against German strongholds in the northern theatre of operations. At first it was planned to strike Kirkenes, Vadsø and Vardö within one day. The aircraft of mine-torpedo aviation regiments were to strike the coastal facilities (warehouses were the

Airacobras of the Northern Fleet Air Force.

main targets), while the attack aircraft were to suppress anti-aircraft artillery and to attack ships and boats in harbours.

Vadsø and Vardö had already been struck by the Northern Fleet Air Force before, but by August 1944, the Northern Fleet Air Force command, knowing that Soviet aviation had caused serious damage to Kirkenes, assumed that German transport ships began to deliver supplies to Vadsø and Vardö, from where they were believed to be transported by small ships to German units on the coast of occupied Finland. However, this was far from the case. Despite all the destruction, Kirkenes remained the main port of supply for the German grouping in the Northern theatre of operations.

The plans of attack on Kirkenes on 23 August were abandoned because of the low cloud cover. However, the weather was fine over Vadsø and Vardö. The plan of attack on Vadsø involved nine groups of bombers and attack aircraft, but as the Kittyhawks did not take part in the fighting over Vadsø, they will not be considered in detail here. In addition to the groups that were supposed to attack Vadsø directly, there were three more groups assigned to cover the attack.

The first, consisting of 16 Airacobras of the 2nd GKAP and eight Kittyhawk fighter-bombers of the 78th IAP, was to block the Luostari airfield. The Kittyhawks were to carry bombs; after bombing, they would join the Airacobras and jointly block the airfield.

The second group, consisting of eight Kittyhawks of the 78th IAP fighter-bombers, was to suppress the German coastal batteries that kept firing at Pummanki.

The third group consisted of the Catalina rescue flying boat, covered by six Kittyhawks and four Airacobras. Looking ahead, it did not have to rescue anyone due to the lack of casualties, but according to the commanders, "the presence of such an aircraft greatly improved the morale of the personnel". Just in case, to avoid problems with the rescue, as had happened on 17 August, the Soviet base on the Sredniy Peninsula was supposed to allocate boats for rescuing pilots from ditched aircraft.

The operation was launched by Kittyhawk fighter-bombers and Airacobras that flew out to block the Luostari airfield. Sixteen Airacobras of the 2nd GKAP (leader – Major I.M. Sukhomlin) together with eight Kittyhawk fighter-bombers of the 78th IAP (leader – Captain V.P. Strelnikov) arrived at Luostari around 12:15. The fighter-bombers dropped their bombs on the airfield. From the combat flight log of the 6th IAD: "At 12:15, the aircraft dropped bombs on Luostari airfield from a dive, from an altitude of 1,500m. As a result, 10 bombs exploded on the airfield, the rest of them – near the airfield". German documents confirm that two of the bombs hit the taxiways. After dropping their bombs, the Kittyhawks, together with Airacobras, were engaged in a blockade of the airfield. Luftwaffe fighters of the 10. and 11. *Staffeln* of the JG 5 did not keep them waiting long; as a result, the air battles over the airfield lasted almost thirty minutes. From the combat flight log of the 6th IAD:

> At 12:25, the aircraft were engaged in an air battle against eight to ten Bf 109s near Luostari at an altitude of 2,000–300m. Lieutenant Pavlov shot down one Bf 109, which fell five to six kilometres north-west of Luostari. Junior Lieutenant Guguev shot down one Bf 109, which crashed one to two kilometres north of Luostari. Captain Strelnikov presumably shot down one Bf 109, which fell two kilometres to the north-west of Hill 220.

Based on the results of the air battles, the Northern Fleet Air Force Headquarters credited Guards Captain V.P. Maksimovich, Guards Senior Lieutenants P.D. Romanov and N.G. Golodnikov of the 2nd GKAP, Lieutenant A.S. Pavlov and Junior Lieutenant I.N. Guguev of the 78th IAP with one downed Bf 109 each. Lieutenant E.I. Mizyukov of the 2nd GKAP and Captain V.P. Strelnikov of the 78th IAP credited one presumable victory over a Bf 109 each.

It should be noted that the blockade of the airfield was successful; only a few Luftwaffe fighters reached Vadsø. There were no casualties during the air battle, only one Kittyhawk of Junior Lieutenant N.A. Shustov received several bullet holes in its wings. All the other Kittyhawks and Airacobras were able to return safely to their airfields.

Meanwhile, Bostons of the 5th MTAD and Il-2s of the 46th ShAP of the 14th SAD bombed Vadsø. The result of their attack is well described in the combat log of the Kirkenes Naval Defence Commander:

> 12:50–13:20, Vadsø. Air raid (by 90 aircraft) carried out in several waves on the town and harbour, 150–200 fragmentation and incendiary bombs dropped. The piers are partly destroyed or damaged… There is a large fire in the city centre (about 70 houses on fire). Numerous military barracks and buildings, including the harbour master's quarters, are destroyed. The electric power station is destroyed. The bridge to Vadsø Island has been hit by a bomb, and the traffic is interrupted. Navy casualties: one dead, six lightly wounded.

Attack aircraft of the 46th ShAP that struck the ships in the port managed to destroy the self-propelled barge B.264.Pmot and the motorship *Hoendip* (194grt). In addition, the high-speed landing barge F-232 and the patrol ship V-6702 were damaged by the strike. None of the Soviet aircraft were shot down during the Vadsø attack. Only a Pe-3 reconnaissance aircraft of the 118th RAP lost contact with the fighters escorting it and was attacked by Bf 109s. As a result, it was damaged, but managed to land at Pummanki.

Eight Kittyhawk fighter-bombers of the 78th IAP bombed the German batteries near Liinahamari, as planned, to ensure the safe landing of Soviet aircraft at Pummanki airfield.

Escorted by fighters, the rescue Catalina flying boat patrolled the harbour, but fortunately there was no work for it.

The individual Luftwaffe fighters who managed to fly in to intercept the aircraft tried to attack the Soviet aircraft, but were unsuccessful everywhere, except for the case with the reconnaissance Pe-3. Following the results of these actions, the Northern Fleet Air Force Headquarters credited one downed Bf 109 to Senior Lieutenant P.M. Kuznetsov of the 20th IAP.

Not limiting itself to the attack on Vadsø, the Soviet command launched a second attack, this time on Vardö. The plan of attack resembled the plan of attack on Vadsø, but there were eight attacking groups. In addition to the groups that directly attacked Vardö, as in the attack on Vadsø, several groups provided support and cover to the attackers. Luostari airfield was to be blocked by 20 Airacobras of the 2nd GKAP and 10 Kittyhawk fighter-bombers of the 78th IAP. Eight Kittyhawk fighter-bombers of the 78th IAP were to suppress the German coastal batteries firing at Pummanki and ensure the safe landing of Soviet aircraft. An additional special group consisted of the rescue Catalina under cover of six Kittyhawks and four Airacobras. Similar to the morning attack, the participation of this group was fortunately limited to boosting the morale of the aircraft crews.

The operation against Vardö was started by the group blocking Luostari airfield. At 16:55, the Kittyhawk fighter-bombers of the 78th IAP (leader – Captain V.P. Strelnikov) were the first to take off and fly to the Ura-Guba airfield to meet the Airacobras of the

2nd GKAP. At 17:10, 20 Airacobras (leader – Guards Lieutenant Colonel M.V. Semenikhin) took off, gathered in a large circle and, after joining with the group of Kittyhawks, followed along the route Ura-Guba – Kuirk Javr Lake – Luostari. The Kittyhawks group was in front, with the Airacobras covering the rear and sides. On the approach to Lake Chapr the Kittyhawk group entered a large cumulus-type cloud. Given the presence of young pilots in the group, the group commander decided to drop their bombs. The Airacobra pilots observed the bombs explode six kilometres south-east of Luostari airfield.

At 17:25, 20 Airacobras of the 2nd GKAP appeared over the airfield. Three groups of Luftwaffe fighters consisting of up to 18 aircraft of the 10. and 11. *Staffeln* of the JG 5 tried to attack the Airacobras and several air combats ensued. As a result of these actions, the Northern Fleet Air Force Headquarters credited one downed Bf 109 to Guards Captains N.A. Bokiy and P.L. Kolomiets, and Guards Lieutenant E.I. Gredyushko each. Documents found in German archives have confirmed the loss of one fighter. It is Bf 109G-6, W.Nr. 411768, tactical number 'Black 1', piloted by *Feldwebel* Willy Schlammer of the 11./JG 5 who was missing in action. Later the body of the pilot was washed ashore by the sea. One Airacobra of the 2nd GKAP did not return from the air battle over Luostari. Its pilot, Guards Lieutenant E.I. Mizyukov, was killed. It should be noted that the 2nd GKAP completely fulfilled its combat mission. None of the strike groups saw any Luftwaffe fighters over Vardö.

Meanwhile, the attack groups struck Vardö. The outcome of the strike as described in German documents:

> 17:45–17:58, Vardö. Air raid (by about 80 aircraft) carried out in three waves. The piers and wharfs were heavily damaged, partly destroyed by the bomb explosions. 142 houses burned down in the town. Three Norwegian motorboats have been sunk. Steamship *Haussa* sustained insignificant damage from cannon and machine-gun fire. Losses of Wehrmacht: eight dead (including the commander of the motor minesweeper R-305), eight seriously and some lightly wounded. According to the Vardö anti-aircraft battery, it shot down three Soviet aircraft, and four more Soviet aircraft were shot down by Luftwaffe fighters.

The Northern Fleet Air Force sustained no losses over Vardö, all aircraft returned to their home airfields. The Luftwaffe pilots, who made 69 combat flights during 23 August 1944, did not suffer from shyness as usual, and claimed 24 downed Soviet aircraft. In fact, they fought mostly against the Luostari blockade fighters of the 2nd GKAP and the 78th IAP. The Northern Fleet Air Force lost one aircraft that day. The Luftwaffe fighter losses known to date amounted to one aircraft.

Kittyhawk fighter-bombers again dropped bombs on the coastal batteries near Liinahamari, and these, according to the pilots, did not fire for the entire time the Kittyhawks were patrolling over them.

The Catalina was circling around Vardö with its escort, but fortunately it did not have to rescue anyone.

The operation was ended by the Pe-3 reconnaissance aircraft of the 118th RAP which photographed the port of Vardö after the strike. The Pe-3 crew had already photographed the town and the port before the attack and were now capturing it after the attack, at the same time looking around carefully for Luftwaffe fighters. But thanks to Airacobras of the 2nd GKAP and Kittyhawks of the 78th IAP, no Luftwaffe fighters appeared.

September 1944

In September, the 78th IAP, the only remaining fighter-bomber regiment, began conducting sensitive strikes against coastal shipping.

In September 1944, the 78th IAP made 331 combat flights, 124 of which were directed against ships and convoys. The fighter-bombers also targeted the enemy coastal facilities: 45 missions were against the enemy artillery batteries, 22 – to strike the enemy front lines, and another 10 – against the enemy bases.

The Northern Fleet Air Force Headquarters credited two downed Bf 109s and one FW 190 to the regiment's pilots. Aircraft losses amounted to five Kittyhawks, all from enemy action. Three pilots did not return from the combat missions.

13 September

On the afternoon of 13 September 1944, the Kittyhawks achieved their first success. Four fighter-bombers (leader – Captain V.P. Strelnikov) flew on a 'free hunting' mission in Varanger Fjord. From the combat flight log of the 6th IAD:

> At 13:10, we carried out a strike on enemy patrol ships using the skip-bombing method with simultaneous machine-gun fire from an altitude of 25m, distance 150m. As a result of the bombing, one FAB-100 hit a patrol ship causing it to sink in the Komagver area.

According to the pilots' reports, Lieutenant A.S. Pavlov achieved one hit on the boat. According to Norwegian historians, the motorboat *Ostervold* was hit. It was damaged by one bomb, but it did not explode. One person in the crew was injured. The ship, having sustained damage, made it to Vadsø.

Captain V.P. Strelnikov, Hero of the Soviet Union.

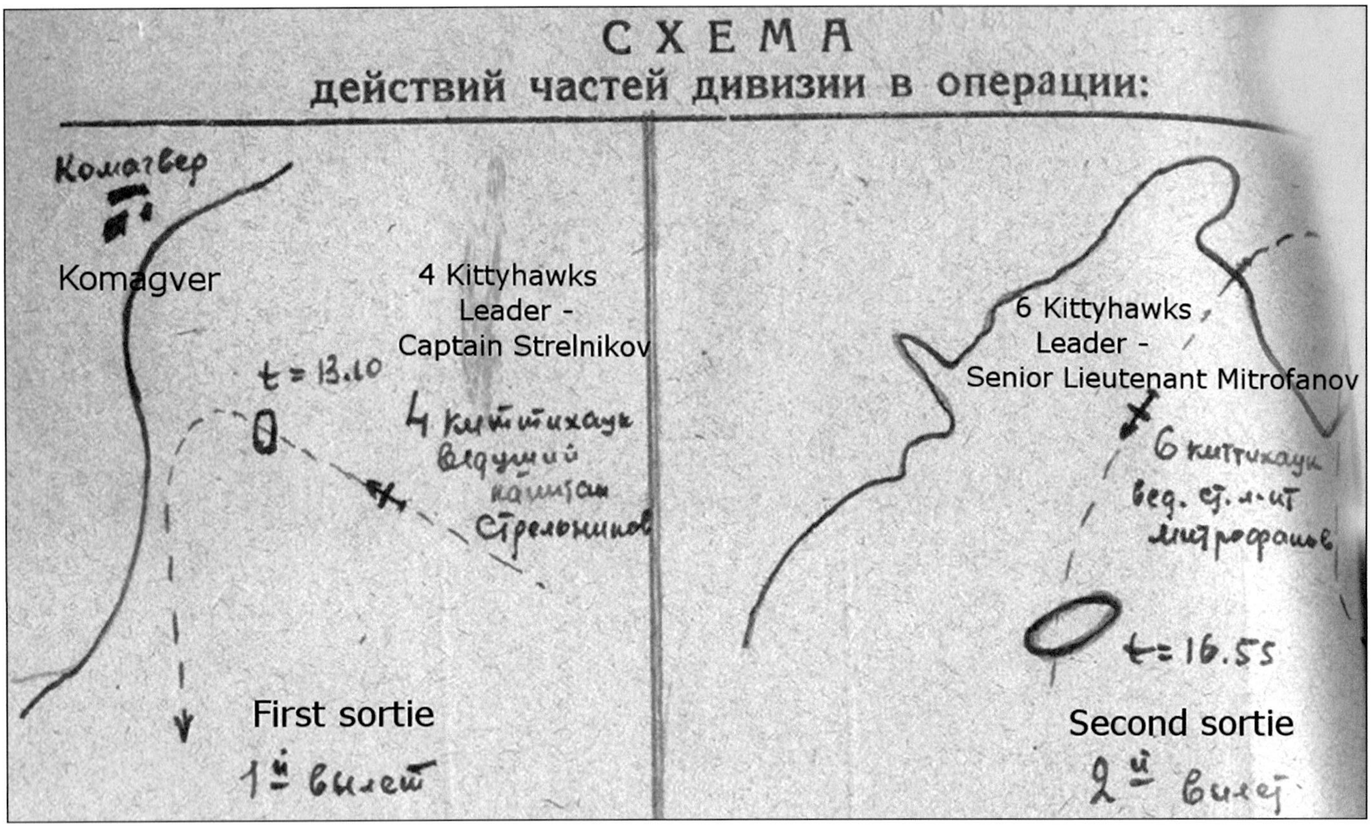

Plan of attack by Kittyhawks of the 78th IAP on 13 September 1944.

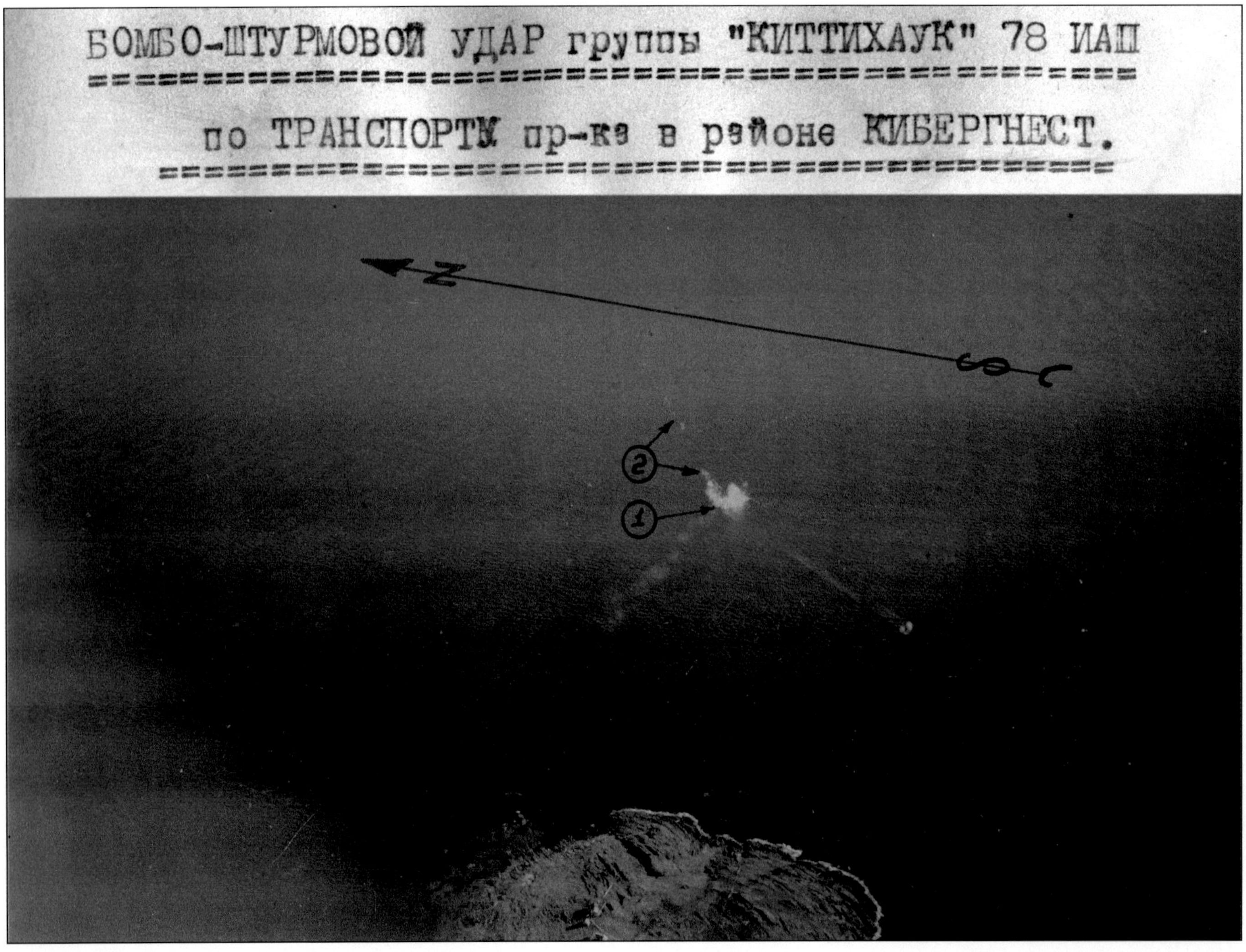

Kittyhawks of the 78th IAP sinking the German coastal ship *Albatros* on 13 September 1944.

P-40K of the 78th IAP. This fighter-bomber dropped FAB-250 bombs using a skip-bombing method during the strikes on Kirkenes in October 1944.

P-40N of the 78th IAP, Rosta airfield, October 1944.

A-20B of the 9th GMTAP, winter 1943–1944.

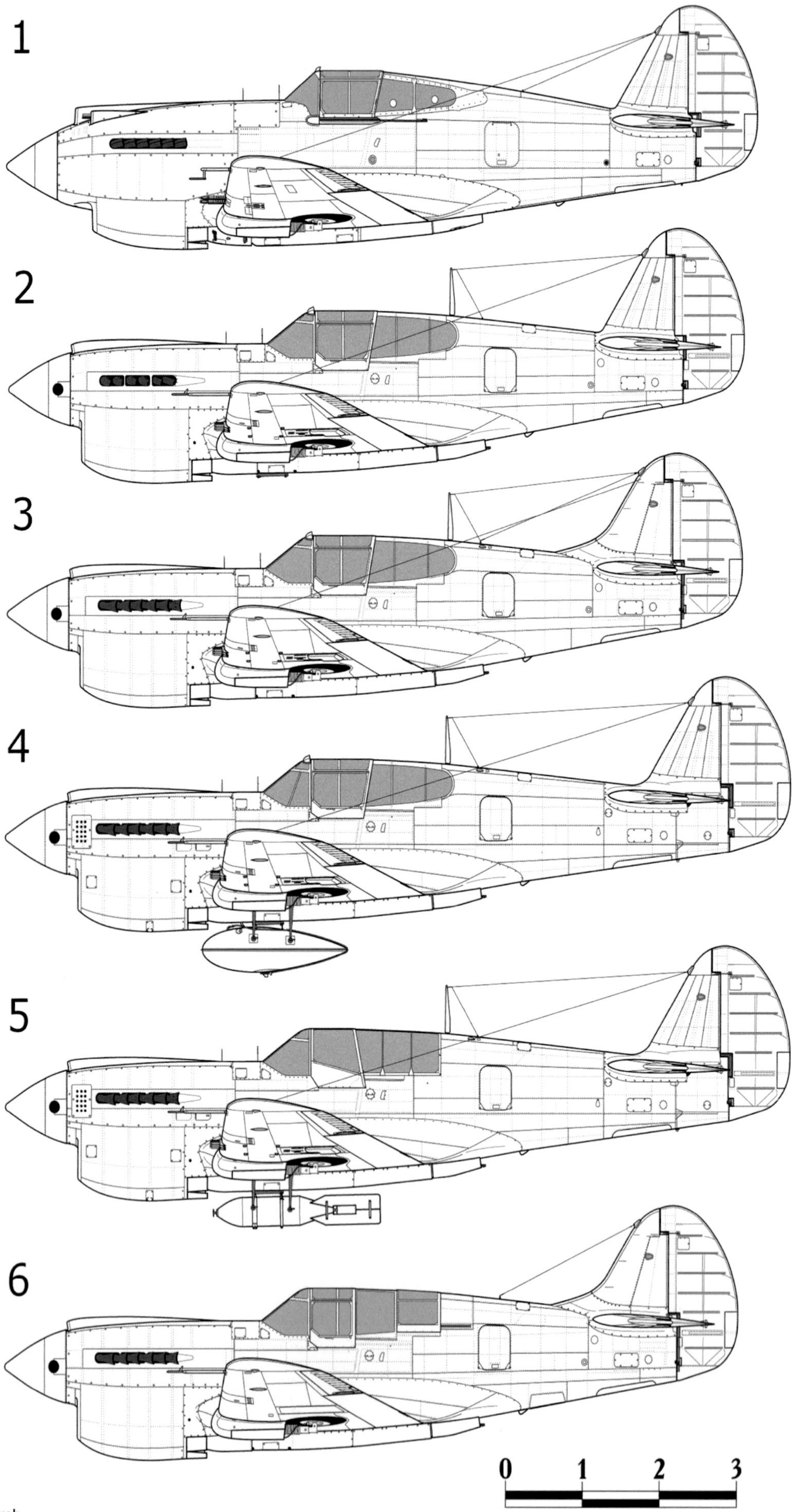

1. Tomahawk IIB (P-40C)
2. P-40E
3. P-40K
4. P-40M with belly tank
5. P-40N5 with FAB-250 bomb
6. P-40EF

A few hours later, six Kittyhawks (leader – Senior Lieutenant V.G. Mitrofanov) sank the first ship in September 1944. From the report of Senior Lieutenant V.G. Mitrofanov:

> Take-off at 16:13, flying at low altitude along the route Rosta – Set-Navolok – Tsyp-Navolok – Vaitolahti – Indre Kiberg Cape. The aircraft attacked a transport ship at 16.55 at Indre Kiberg Cape. My bombs fell three to five metres near the transport. Baev's bombs hit the target. Other bombs fell with undershoot.

According to German documents, at 16:55, near Kibergnes Cape, 'six Il-2s' sank the German coastal ship *Albatros* (119grt), which was sailing with military cargo. The ship was armed with one 20mm anti-aircraft gun. The attack resulted in the death of three German servicemen, including the anti-aircraft gun crew. Sixteen men were rescued by an approaching motor minesweeper. From the available data it can be concluded that it was the Junior Lieutenant I.M. Baev who succeeded in hitting the motor ship with two bombs, resulting in its destruction. Some historians believe that the motor ship was a minesweeper, but recent research shows that at the time of its destruction this ship was not part of the Kriegsmarine and was an ordinary transport vessel.

14 September

The first to succeed that day was the group of four Kittyhawks, led by Captain V.P. Strelnikov. From the report of Captain B.P. Strelnikov:

> Take-off at 8:45, flying at low altitude along the route Rosta – Set-Navolok – Tsyp-Navolok – Vaitolahti – Vardö – Makkaur-Sann Fjord. The aircraft attacked two minesweepers in Makkaur-Sann Fjord which were heading at a 110-degree course. Time of the attack: 9:40. After the attack I observed a hit from my two FAB-100s. The bombs penetrated the deck and exploded at the port side. Lieutenant Grigoriev's bombs [the strike was done by the skip-bombing method – Author's note] hit the starboard side and other bombs fell with undershoot. The minesweeper halted, emitting smoke from the stern. The aircraft sustained heavy anti-aircraft fire in the target area.

According to German documents, two patrol ships, V-6104 and V-6115, which were heading for Kirkenes from Smålfjord after convoying transports, were hit by Kittyhawks in Makkaur Sand Fjord. As a result of the attack, eight bombs exploded around V-6104, causing light damage to the ship's engine. The vessel's commander and two soldiers on board were wounded by bomb splinters and machine-gun fire. The combat log of the 61st Patrol Boats Flotilla records that the crew of the ship counted about 50 holes in her sides resulting from machine-gun fire. The command of the 6th IAD believed that the ship was sunk, but the Northern Fleet Air Force Headquarters decided that the minesweeper was only damaged by Captain V.P. Strelnikov and Second Lieutenant P.G. Grigoriev.

Sometime later, at 12:45, four Kittyhawk fighter-bombers and a pair of Kittyhawks (with cameras for monitoring the attack results) of the 78th IAP (leader – Senior Lieutenant A.Ya. Shvailakh) flew to Varanger Fjord for a 'free-hunting' mission under the cover of four Airacobras of the 2nd GKAP. From the combat flight log of the 6th IAD:

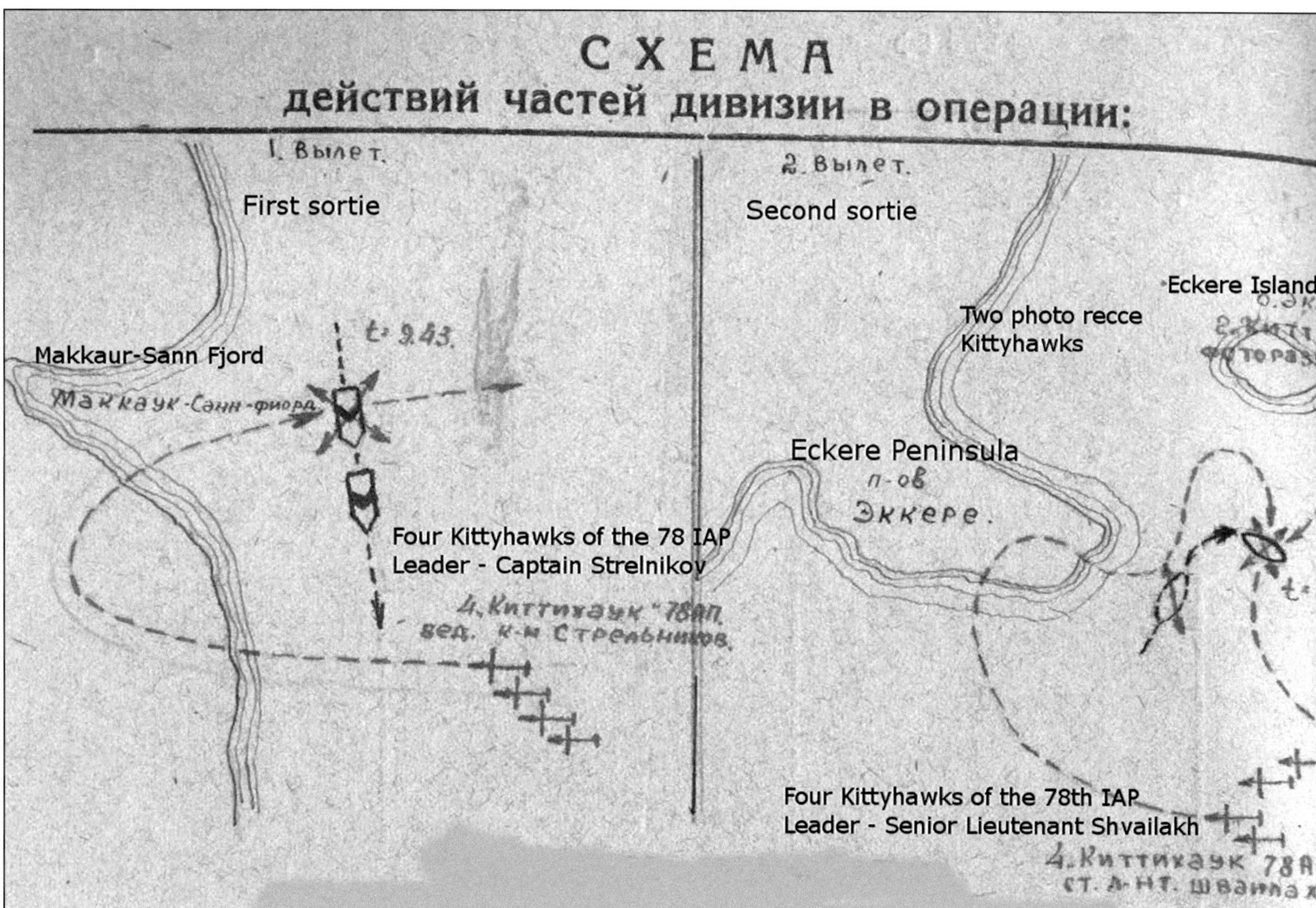

Plan of attack by Kittyhawks of the 78th IAP on 14 September 1944.

> At 13:25, near Eckerö, the aircraft struck a 100-tonne motorboat of patrol type, using the skip-bombing method from an altitude of 25m and distance of 150-200m, simultaneously firing machine guns at it. As a result of the bombing, the motorboat caught fire and sank.

According to German documents, the missing motorboat *Borgheim* (V-73) was hit and did indeed catch fire and sink. The attack resulted in the death of one German soldier and one Norwegian sailor. The Northern Fleet Air Force Headquarters credited the sinking of the motorboat to Junior Lieutenant V.I. Volkov. One Kittyhawk was shot down by anti-aircraft fire from the Eckerö coastal battery while photographing the results of the attack. According to the report of the pilots involved in the attack: "From a direct hit by an anti-aircraft artillery shell, the aircraft caught fire and fell into the sea". Its pilot, Junior Lieutenant P.F. Rezanovich, was killed.

15 September

The day began with an unsuccessful attack on a small German convoy. At 1:55, a convoy consisting of patrol ship *Togo* and motor lighter MW-35 with the Finnish patrol ship *Turja* in tow started from Petsamo. In addition to them, the convoy also included 12 motor minesweepers. At about 6:45, the torpedo boats Nos. 114, 213, 214, 216 and 241 attacked the convoy, but did not succeed. Four Kittyhawks of the 78th IAP, which covered them from the air, tried to assist the torpedo boats by striking the German ships, but lost one aircraft without achieving any success. From the accident report on the loss of the aircraft: "Supporting the attack by the torpedo boats, a group of Kittyhawks fired machine-guns at the escort ships which were counteracting our torpedo boats. During the strike, one aircraft was hit by anti-aircraft fire from the convoy's escort ships. Due to the impossibility of reaching the airfield, the pilot ditched in the water and was rescued by the torpedo boats." The pilot, Lieutenant D.I. Muromtsev, was not injured.

At 7:30, near the entrance to Beck Fjord the patrol ship *Turja* broke off. As a result, four ships lagged behind the convoy while a new tug was being attached. Lichter MW-35 tried to start the new tug, but failed. Similarly futile were the attempts to attach the tug by the motor minesweeper R-154. While the two ships were fiddling with the tugs, the motor minesweeper R-202 was providing cover. At 7:44, six Il-2s of the 46th ShAP (leader – Senior Lieutenant V.M. Skopintsev) attacked the German ships under cover of six Yak-7s of the 20th IAP. In the course of the attack, one bomb fell near the port side of the motor minesweeper R-202 and another exploded in the wake from the same minesweeper, but they did not inflict any damage. After the attack by a group of Il-2s, the Germans managed to attach a tug to tow the patrol boat and continued to move towards Kirkenes.

Around 8:00, Bf 109s of the 7./JG 5 tried to attack torpedo boats which were leaving after the attack on the convoy but were stopped by the Soviet fighters. In the air combats that followed Guards Lieutenant N.G. Golodnikov of the 2nd GKAP was credited with two Bf 109s, Captain P.I. Sakharov of the 78th IAP one Bf 109, and Senior Lieutenant V.S. Shevchenko of the 20th IAP one Bf 109 as well. German documents confirm that two aircraft were lost:

- Bf 109G-6, W.Nr. 166117, tactical number 'Black 5'. The pilot, *Leutnant* Günther Fuhrmann, was reported missing after this battle;
- Bf 109G-6, W.Nr. 412439. The pilot, *Unteroffizier* Heinz Lork, was wounded but managed to bail out.

The Luftwaffe pilots claimed to have shot down seven Soviet aircraft during the battle. In fact, two Airacobras of the 2nd GKAP did not return from the mission. Their pilots, Guards Lieutenant P.A. Kukhlivskiy and Guards Senior Technician-Lieutenant A.I. Shevchenko, were missing. Some documents of the 2nd GKAP state that they were not shot down, but collided in course of the air battle.

At 8:45, two groups of attack aircraft struck a group of ships towing the patrol boat *Turja*. The first group consisted of six skip-bombing Il-2s of the 46th ShAP (leader – Senior Lieutenant M.M. Tamarov) under the cover of six Airacobras of the 27th IAP. The second group also consisted of six Il-2s (leader – Lieutenant N.I. Khilinskiy) covered by six Yak-7Bs of the 20th IAP, but they attacked the enemy ships from a dive. Alas, despite the combined attack, there was no success. The German ships were again unharmed. On the contrary, the Soviet side suffered losses, not because of enemy action, but because of the unpredictable northern weather. By the time of the aircraft's return, fog had fallen over the airfields. As a result, the 46th ShAP lost four Il-2s and three crews, and the 27th IAP lost one Airacobra fighter with its pilot.

However, four hours later the fighter-bombers proved that they could hit the target. At 12:25, four Kittyhawk fighter-bombers of the 78th IAP (leader – Lieutenant A.S. Pavlov) took off on a 'free-hunting' mission in the Varanger Fjord under the cover of four Airacobras of the 2nd GKAP. At 13:05, the group spotted near Kiberg what the pilots first thought was a 'tanker'. At 13:10, the Kittyhawks dropped bombs on the target using the skip-bombing method. From the report of Lieutenant A.S. Pavlov:

> A tanker of about 10,000 tonnes displacement was attacked near the islands five to seven kilometres south of Kibergnes. I observed a direct hit by four FAB-100s. My bombs exploded in the aft part of the ship. Dzyuba 's bombs undershot by two to three metres and exploded in the middle of the ship. Baev's bombs exploded behind the ship. The tanker slowed down and listed. Sinking was not observed. At the exit of the attack, we were subjected to anti-aircraft machine-gun fire.

Most unexpectedly, the other pilots of the group also made the mistake of taking the high-speed landing barge for a tanker. From the report of Lieutenant D.P. Dzyuba:

> A tanker with a displacement of 5,000–7,000 tonnes was attacked south of Kibergnes near three islands. I observed a direct hit of two FAB-100 bombs, dropped by Lieutenant Pavlov, in the aft of the ship. My bombs were two to three metres under. They exploded in the central part of the tanker. Bombs dropped by Lieutenant Baev undershot by five to six metres. The tanker lost speed, its aft part settled into the water with a list to the right. During the attack we were fired at by the enemy's anti-aircraft artillery … The aircraft flown by Lieutenant Pavlov was hit, a shell hit the stabilizer and the propeller.

The Kittyhawks struck a high-speed landing barge F-232A, carrying 80 tonnes of disassembled barracks to Svartnes.[1] The engines of the

1 Historical note: High-speed landing barge F-232A was built at Gebr. Müller shipyard, Foxhol. Construction was started on 12 May 1941. In April 1942, it entered service and was part of the 21st Landing Ship Flotilla. Standard displacement – 155 tonnes, full displacement – 220 tonnes. Length – 47m, width – 6.5m, draft – 1.5m. The cruising speed was 10.5 knots. Crew – 21. On 18 September 1944 it was towed to Vadsø. At the beginning of October, the barge was towed for repairs to Kirkenes, where it was sunk (near Neiden) on 26 October 1944 when German forces were leaving the port.

barge failed due to the direct hits and close bomb explosions, and the ship was grounded. According to the report of the mechanical engineer of the landing flotilla, one bomb penetrated the barge from port to starboard 20cm above the waterline. Two other bombs hit the port side 10cm below the waterline. Another bomb fell astern on the starboard side, and the explosion caused all three engines to emit smoke. In addition to the damage from the bombs, the barge was damaged by machine-gun fire. The barge listed to the port side, so that it drew water through the ramp. The crew lost one man killed and three wounded.

The fact that the attacked target was not a tanker was not immediately established. At 15:35, a pilot of an Airacobra of the 2nd GKAP, Guards Senior Lieutenant V.I. Mukhin, carried out a reconnaissance mission of the damaged ship two to three kilometres to the south of Kibergnes Cape. From the report of V.I. Mukhin:

> A mission to reconnoitre strike results. Take off at 15:15. The target was found at 15:35. I observed a ship two to three kilometres south of Kibergnes Cape (it looked like a tanker up to 3,000 tonnes displacement) to the south-east towards Vaitolahti listing to the starboard side. The starboard side was 1–1.5m off the water (roll 45–50 degrees). The bow was pointing towards Kibergnes Cape, no movement on board, no one was near the vessel. No encounters with enemy aircraft. Anti-aircraft guns did not fire.

The reconnaissance aircraft took a photo survey, and on the basis of the photos the Fleet Air Force Headquarters credited the damage to the self-propelled barge to Lieutenant A.S. Pavlov. It should be noted that F-232A was never repaired after the damage sustained in this attack.

Meanwhile, it was decided to finish off this 'tanker' and a group of six Kittyhawk fighter-bombers of the 78th IAP (leader – Captain V.P. Strelnikov) under the cover of six Airacobras of the 2nd GKAP (leader – Captain P.D. Klimov) was sent. The group did not find the 'tanker' and at 16:05 attacked the port of Eckerö. According to the observations of the pilots, the bombs hit warehouses; pilots Lieutenants P.G. Grigoriev and I.N. Guguev reported the sinking of two motorboats. The sinking of the motorboats was not credited by the Northern Fleet Air Force Headquarters because the destruction of the target was not confirmed by photographic evidence. German documents state that the strike by Kittyhawks resulted in damages to the port and sinking of one motorboat. On the return route, one Airacobra of the 2nd GKAP crashed into the sea and sank due to a maneuvering error. Its pilot, Guards Senior Lieutenant M.M. Chepurnov, was killed. The dead body was picked up from the lifeboat by the crew of the Catalina rescue aircraft.

Meanwhile, the attack aircraft of the 46th ShAP found a more interesting target. Earlier in the morning the Bostons of the 36th MTAP attacked the transports in the port of Berlevåg. Later, the Northern Fleet Air Force command decided to involve the attack aircraft of the 46th IAP and Kittyhawk fighter-bombers of the 78th IAP based at the Pummanki airfield in the strike on the transports in the same port.

At 15:35, five Il-2s of the 46th ShAP (leader – Major D.V. Osyka), eight Kittyhawk fighter-bombers of the 78th IAP (leader – Captain P.I. Sakharov), six Yak-7 fighters (leader – Senior Lieutenant K.V. Boychenko) and four Airacobras of the 20th IAP (leader – Captain A.K. Tarasov) took off from Pummanki.

At 16:21, the fighter-bombers attacked the port of Berlevåg and the attack aircraft struck the 'transports' in the port of Berlevåg using the skip-bombing method. The report of the fighter pilot of the 20th IAP, Lieutenant I.P. Sarafanov notes:

> I report that while escorting five Il-2s striking enemy ships in the Berlevåg Bay, on the approach to the target I saw two transports and several escort ships. After the attack of the Il-2s, I saw one hit in the bow of a transport ship with a displacement of 8,000–9,000 tonnes, the bow of which was seen submerged in water when I was leaving the target. A second hit in the same transport was observed near the starboard side. A large explosion was observe … Several hits with undershoot and

Plan of attack on the high-speed landing barge by a group of Kittyhawks of the 78th IAP on 15 September 1944.

Photo reconnaissance report of the results of the air strike on the German convoy on 15 September 1944.

> overshoot were near a transport with a displacement of 6,000–7,000 tonnes, which in my opinion remained unharmed as it remained in the same position on the water's surface. I saw a direct hit by a Kittyhawk on the pier, which probably burned up. A number of large explosions from Kittyhawk attacks were observed in the area of the storage facilities.

The submarine hunter UJ-1224 was sunk by the strike of attack aircraft. The fighter-bombers had nothing to do with its destruction.

16 September

At 7:55, five fighter-bombers and one photo reconnaissance Kittyhawks of the 78th IAP (leader – Senior Lieutenant A.I. Batrakov) left for 'free hunting' mission in Varanger Fjord. From the combat flight log of the 6th IAD:

> No enemy ships were observed on the enemy's lines of communication in Varanger Fjord. 08:35. A skip-bombing attack was carried out from an altitude of 25m at a distance of 150–200m on a reserve target – the port of Kibergnes. The strike damaged the pier, set fire to two residential buildings, and destroyed a warehouse.

According to German data, in the course of this attack, the motorboat *Fremtiden* (15grt) was sunk by a direct bomb hit. As the crew was on shore, no casualties were sustained. On the same day, an accident occurred in the 118th RAP. During a night training flight, a Kittyhawk reconnaissance aircraft went off-course on take-off and crashed into a hillside. The pilot, Lieutenant N.F. Shvets, was killed.

17 September

Five fighter-bombers and one photo reconnaissance Kittyhawks of the 78th IAP (leader – Captain V.P. Strelnikov) flew on a 'free hunting' mission against individual targets between Vardö and Makkaur Cape. From the report of Captain V.P. Strelnikov:

> Take-off at 6:07. Rosta – Set-Navolok – Tsyp-Navolok – Vaitolahti – north of Vardö 10–15km to Makkaur Cape. Flying at low altitude up to Pers Fjord, further on with climb up to 1,100m. At 6:55, at Makkaur Cape I attacked a self-propelled barge that was ahead in the wake of two self-propelled barges, 120 degrees course, speed 10–12 knots, displacement 600–700 tonnes. I observed two of my FAB-100s hitting the aft of the self-propelled barge. As a result of the explosion, the barge rolled to starboard and took on water to the stern. The barge turned towards the shore and lost speed. The second barge continued on the same course. Final sinking could not be observed, as my wingman, Junior Lieutenant Grigoriev, had a malfunctioning of his aircraft engine. I observed Junior Lieutenant Baev suppressing two anti-aircraft machine guns

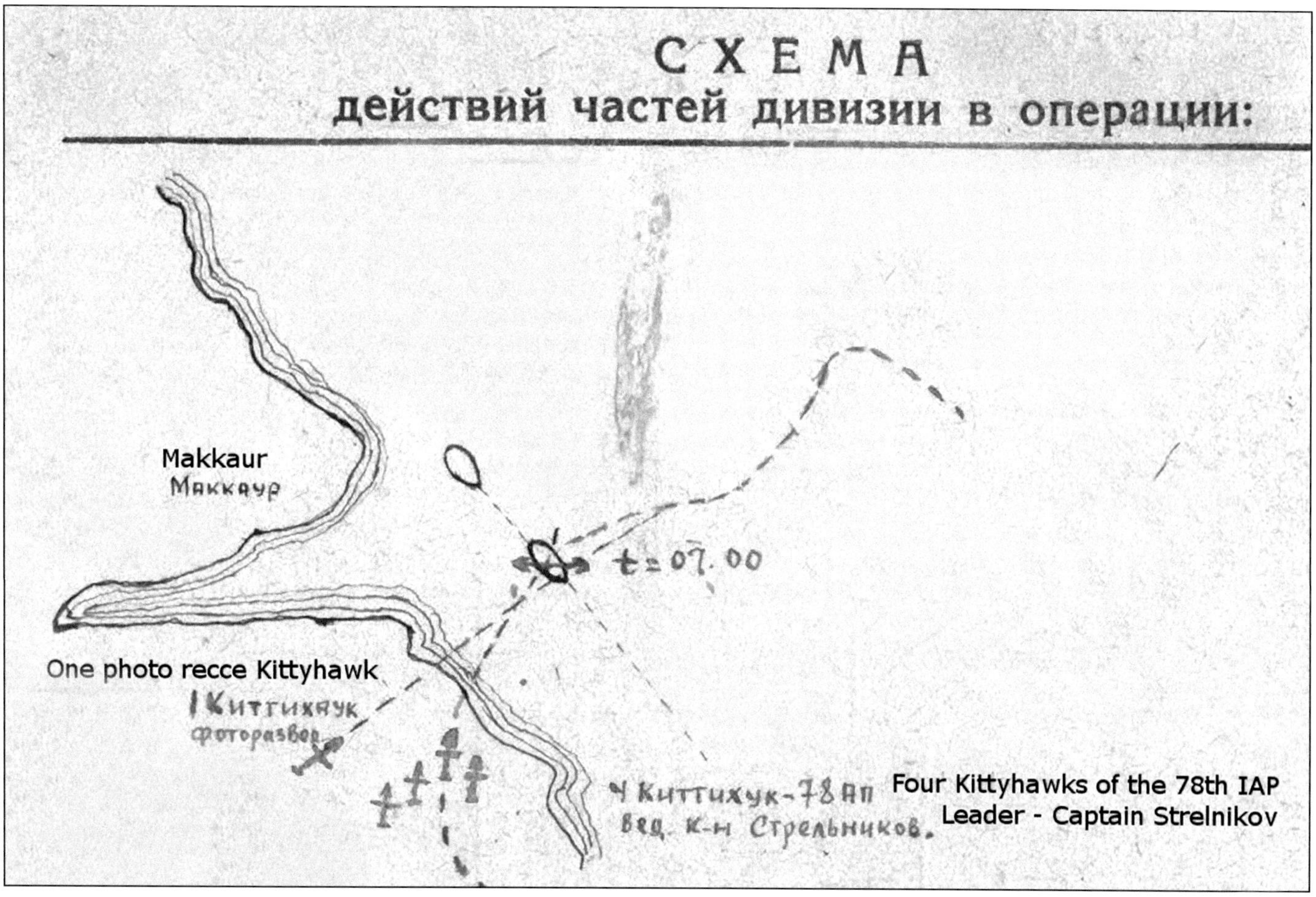

Plan of attack on two high-speed landing barges by Kittyhawks of the 78th IAP on 17 September 1944.

> on the damaged transport and Lieutenant Dzyuba striking the one on the hill; the machine guns were firing at me when I was attacking.

According to the reports of the pilots involved in the attack, apart from Captain V.P. Strelnikov, no one hit the German ships with the bombs. From the German documents it is known that two high-speed landing barges, F-196 and F-209, were attacked. The first one was hit by two bombs and caught fire, which the Germans extinguished with great difficulty. The Northern Fleet Air Force Headquarters credited Captain V.P. Strelnikov with the damage to a high-speed landing barge.

19 September

At 14:25 eight fighter-bombers and two photo reconnaissance Kittyhawks of the 78th IAP (leader – Senior Lieutenant A.Ya. Shvailakh) took off from Rosta airfield and 20 minutes later were joined by eight Airacobras of the 2nd GKAP (leader – Captain N.M. Didenko), after which the group set out to attack the enemy ships in the Komagnes area. From the combat flight log of the 6th IAD:

> 15:05. The aircraft conducted a strike using a skip-bombing method from an altitude of 20–25m from 200m distance and simultaneously fired machine guns at a minesweeper. On development of the [reconnaissance] photos one direct bomb hit was seen on the bow of the minesweeper and one hit two to three metres away from the same vessel. The target was damaged. There were no encounters with enemy fighters.

Due to the absence of enemy fighters, Airacobras also took part in the attack, firing their cannon and machine guns at the German ships. Five motor minesweepers of the 21st Motor Minesweepers Flotilla were hit. From the combat log:

> 15:15. Air alert, attacked by about 20 Il-2s, bombs and machine-gun fire. At 15:18, trawls were cut off, at 15:20 the attack was over. Damage report: R-308 has a dent in the armour on the bridge from the port side – apparently ricochet of a bomb. There are 12 holes in the hull from cannon and machine-gun fire and from bomb splinters, the starboard engine is out of action. R-307 has 13 holes in the bridge and upper deck from cannon and machine-gun fire and from bomb splinters. The crew have four men, including the commander, wounded.

As a result of the Kittyhawks attack, the motor minesweeper R-308 went to Kirkenes for repairs. Interestingly, German army documents say that the attack was unsuccessful. Eight more Airacobras of the 2nd GKAP flew to cut off the Luftwaffe fighters, but there was no enemy in the air.

25 September

On this day the fighter-bombers took part in another battle against a German convoy. This was convoy Lf.133.Ki, which sailed from Lo Fjord to Kirkenes on 24 September. It consisted of patrol boats V-6105, V-6107, V-6110, motor minesweeper R-160, high-speed landing barge/floating workshop F-152.W, and transport *Gothia* (1,972grt). On the way, *Gothia* went into port, and the patrol ship V-6101 joined the convoy.

On the morning of 25 September the convoy was spotted by a pair of Yak-7Bs of the 20th IAP, after which torpedo boats and aircraft were directed at the convoy. Nine torpedo boats left at night to attack the convoy. At about 10:00, the Northern Fleet Air Force sent 58 aircraft including 20 attack aircraft, to strike the convoy.

Around 10:45, the attacking aircraft and torpedo boats struck the convoy. After receiving two hits by torpedoes and two by bombs, the patrol ship V-6101 sank. It was followed by steamer *Inno II* (150grt), that was unlucky to be sailing in the area of the attack on the convoy. The attack aircraft succeeded in hitting the ship with their bombs, and it sank instantly.

During the retreat after attacking the convoy, the torpedo boats were attacked by Luftwaffe FW 190 fighter-bombers, which managed to seriously damage torpedo boat TKA-242. The Northern Fleet Air Force command responded by ordering fighters to cover the retreating torpedo boats.

After the torpedo boats and attack aircraft, convoy Lf.133.Ki was struck by fighter-bombers of the 78th IAP. At 11:50, a dozen Kittyhawk fighter-bombers carrying one FAB-250 each, a pair of Kittyhawk reconnaissance aircraft and a wing of Kittyhawk fighters from 78th IAP (leader – Major V.I. Babernov) attacked the convoy in the area of Eckerö – Scalnes. Two patrol boats (V-6110 and V-6105) and barge/floating workshop F-152.W which was floating near the shore came under attack. Eight Kittyhawks under the command of Captain V.P. Strelnikov missed F-152.W. The reason for the miss was that the Germans were wise enough to run aground. The group of four aircraft led by Senior Lieutenant A.Y. Shvailakh achieved a better result. From the report of Junior Lieutenant L.I. Pustobaev: "I observed two bombs exploding near a transport ship. The latter lost speed and stopped".

The combat log of the 61st Patrol Boats Flotilla records that at 11:52 a bomb exploded a metre away from the starboard side on the traverse of patrol ship V-6105. The ship's engine, rudder, and radio were put out of action. The ship developed a heavy leak and emitted a cloud of steam. As the rudder failed, the ship began to circle, two German crewmembers were thrown overboard and were not picked up. There were two more seriously wounded crewmembers, one of whom died of his wounds. The ship was taken to Sandbuktu with the help of an auxiliary rudder and ran aground at a depth of four metres. On another patrol ship, V-6110, a steam line was damaged by heavy machine-gun fire and the boiler and engine room had to be abandoned, but the ship's steam engine continued to run. The crew lost one man killed and three wounded. The ship entered Sandbuktu and anchored 200m offshore.

A report of the 6th IAD recorded that Senior Lieutenant A.Ya. Shvailakh and Lieutenant N.N. Skrebkov had damaged the 1,500-tonne transport, but the Northern Fleet Air Force Headquarters considered this report unreliable.

Two Kittyhawks were damaged by anti-aircraft fire but returned to their home base. One of the pilots, Senior Lieutenant A.Ya. Shvailakh, was lightly wounded.

Two hours later another attack followed: at 14:15, six Kittyhawk fighter-bombers of the 78th IAP (leader – Senior Lieutenant A.I. Batrakov) attacked the convoy at Eckerö – Scalnes area. According to the German documents, the target of the attack was the convoy and five motor minesweepers which had come to its rescue. Eleven German ships came under attack: two damaged patrol boats, one barge/floating workshop and eight motor minesweepers. The Soviet pilots honestly reported that the bombs did not hit the transport (in fact, it was patrol ship V-6105). The Northern Fleet Air Force Headquarters assessed the strike as unsuccessful, but this was far from the case. All the bombs did miss the ships, but the machine-gun fire was very effective. The engine room on motor minesweeper R-309 caught fire; the bridge and radio set were damaged. The crew of R-309 lost three men killed and seven wounded, including the commander of the ship seriously wounded. The motor minesweeper R-202 reported numerous holes in the deck. Four crew members were wounded.

The German ships managed to shoot down one Kittyhawk during this attack. From the accident report on the loss of the aircraft: "The aircraft was damaged by a direct hit from an anti-aircraft artillery shell. The pilot ditched the aircraft 25–30 kilometres west of the island of Heinia Saari". The badly injured pilot, Junior Lieutenant V.E. Kondrashov, landed on the water and got into a life raft. Information about the ditched aircraft was relayed to the Northern Fleet Air Force Headquarters. At 14:30, torpedo boat TKA-215 was ordered to pick up the pilot behind the Ainovy Islands. At 15:30, together with another boat, it managed to find and pick up the seriously wounded pilot. At 16:10, the two boats were attacked by several Bf 109s. Four Kittyhawks, covering them, engaged in combat and the Northern Fleet Air Force Headquarters credited one downed Bf 109 to Lieutenant A.F. Nikolayev. The Luftwaffe aircraft, according to the pilot's report, went down in the sea in the area 20–25 km east of Eckerö Cape. The Luftwaffe fighters tried to attack the torpedo boats, but achieved nothing. One of the Bf 109s, according to the sailors' report, was hit by the ship's machine gun and crashed on the Sredniy Peninsula. At 16:40, the TKA-215 group arrived at the base. According to Luftwaffe reports, two FW 190 fighter-bombers of *Schlachtgeschwader* 5 tried to attack Soviet torpedo boats, but achieved nothing, losing one FW 190.

Half an hour before TKA-215 arrived at the base, TKA-202 and TKA-208 put out to sea. Their task was to search for Soviet pilots who had ditched their aircraft near Heinesaari Island. The torpedo boats entered the area and carried out a search from 16:25 to 17:00, but failed to find anyone. They were covered by four Kittyhawks of the 78th IAP from the air.

At 16:40, in the search area, the torpedo boats were attacked by four Bf 109s and four FW 190s, but their attack was repulsed by the Kittyhawks. The fighter pilots succeeded in forcing the Luftwaffe fighter-bombers to drop bombs into the sea. Based on the results of the air combat, the Northern Fleet Air Force Headquarters credited one downed FW 190 to Lieutenant V.I. Kirichenko. The torpedo boats were not damaged, but one Kittyhawk was shot down. From the accident report on the loss of aircraft: "While covering TKA, the aircraft was engaged in air combat against two fours of Bf 109s and FW 190s which had broken off into single aircraft while gaining altitude. The aircraft was suddenly attacked from behind and shot down by FW 190 enemy aircraft". The pilot of the aircraft, Junior Lieutenant I.P. Alistratov, was killed. Two other Kittyhawks were seriously damaged, but managed to land at Pummanki airfield. Their pilots, Lieutenant V.V. Venikov and Junior Lieutenant N.A. Shustov, were wounded. The Bf 109s of 13./JG 5 took part in the combat on the enemy side. The Germans claimed two victories without any losses of their own.

Assessing the results of this air combat, the Northern Fleet Air Force Headquarters recommended that the Kittyhawks be covered by Airacobras and Yak-7B fighters.

A most unpleasant event occurred later. After the air combat, the Kittyhawks withdrew to their airfields, apparently without informing the torpedo boats about this fact. As a result, TKA-202 and TKA-208 mistook the Luftwaffe aircraft that attacked them at 17:21 for Soviet fighters and did not take the necessary measures to defend themselves. As a result of the attack both boats were damaged, TKA-202 severely: one sailor was killed and 10 were wounded. According to Luftwaffe reports, eight FW 190 fighter-bombers attacked the torpedo boats and managed to set one of them on fire. While one group of Kittyhawks was covering the torpedo boats, the other group performed a 'cruising' (as the documents of the time say) flight against enemy communication lines. The group consisted of five fighter-bombers and one photo-reconnaissance Kittyhawks of the 78th IAP (leader – Captain V.P. Strelnikov). They succeeded in finding another victim – the motorboat *Ternen* (106grt). From the combat flight log of the 6th IAD:

> At 16:57, near Westerns Cape … [unintelligible] one enemy patrol boat was spotted; the aircraft attacked using a skip-bombing method from an altitude of 25–30m, distance of 200–150m and simultaneously fired machine guns at it. As a result of the direct hit of a FAB-100 bomb dropped by Captain Strelnikov and Senior Lieutenant Mitrofanov, the patrol boat sank.

According to German documents, only one bomb hit the target, but it was more than enough. The motorboat sank, one crew member was killed and another wounded.

Right: Kittyhawks of the Northern Fleet Air Force providing air cover for torpedo boats.

Below: Plan of attack on the convoy Lf.133.Ki by the Kittyhawks on 25 September 1944.

Sinking of the German patrol ship V-6101 on 25 September 1944.

26 September

Attack aircraft of the 46th ShAP made two strikes against German ships and motorboats in the port of Vadsø.

The first strike was successful. At the cost of one aircraft, the attack aircraft succeeded in damaging three high-speed landing barges and a patrol boat. In the air combat, the fighters of the 20th IAP claimed seven victories over Luftwaffe fighters, of which four were confirmed by Luftwaffe documents available to date.

After the successful first strike, the Northern Fleet Air Force command decided to launch a second strike against Vadsø. Two attack groups took part in it, the first from the Vaenga-2 airfield and the second from the Pummanki airfield.

The Vaenga-2 group consisted of six Il-2s of the 46th ShAP (leader – Captain P.A. Yevdokimov) covered by two Airacobras and four Yak-7Bs of the 20th IAP (leader – Lieutenant G.A. Dmitrik) and eight Airacobras of the 27th IAP (leader – Senior Lieutenant V.K. Vashchenko).

The Pummanki airfield group consisted of six Il-2s of the 46th ShAP (leader – Senior Lieutenant V.M. Skopintsev) under the cover of four Yak-7Bs of the 20th IAP (leader – Senior Lieutenant K.V. Boychenko) and four Kittyhawk fighters of the 78th IAP.

At 17:43, both groups of attack aircraft struck the port of Vadsø. From the report of the 5th Landing Ship Flotilla:

> At 16:30, the second attack by 20 aircraft followed, again coming from different directions and diving only at the harbour and ships, while the settlement and the base were attacked with cannon and machine-gun fire. They did not cause any significant damage.

The Norwegians acknowledge the loss of the motorboat T-77-T *Monne* (39grt). At the time of its destruction, it was used by the *Kriegsmarine* Maritime Transport. However, there is no complete clarity about its fate – according to some documents, it was sunk during the first strike by the attack aircraft, others say that it happened during the second attack. It is possible that other motorboats may have also been hit, but there is no comprehensive information about all vessels of this type yet.

The anti-aircraft fire was heavy, and fatal for one Kittyhawk of the 78th IAP. From the accident report on the loss of the aircraft: "While escorting the Il-2s on the bombing strike to Vadse, the aircraft was subjected to anti-aircraft artillery fire in the target area, the engine of the aircraft was hit. On the way back on the traverse of Beck Fjord the aircraft crashed into the sea and sank, the pilot was killed." Junior Lieutenant N.I. Kravchenko did not return from the mission. For a long time, he was listed in all documents as killed in action, but only recently it was established that N.I. Kravchenko was taken prisoner and returned home in May 1945.

Luftwaffe fighters, which took off to intercept the Soviet attack aircraft, did not reach the group. They encountered a group of six Yak-7Bs (leader – Captain E. Petrenko) that had taken off from Pummanki airfield to cut off the enemy aircraft from Soviet aircraft that were returning from a mission to Vadsø. During the air combat the Soviet fighters claimed four victories, while the Luftwaffe fighters two shot-down aircraft. According to information available to date, the Germans lost one Bf 109G-6, tactical number 'Yellow 13', W.Nr. 14630, of the 11./JG 5. The pilot, *Unteroffizier* Heinrich Pflaum, was able to escape the doomed aircraft and float in his inflatable life raft, in which he reached the shore two days later without any help.

Luftwaffe pilots, in their turn, damaged one Yak-7B, whose pilot managed to make an emergency landing at Pummanki airfield. The aircraft was sent for repairs, and the pilot, Lieutenant I.P. Sarafanov, was taken to hospital.

29 September

On this date the fighter-bombers of the 78th IAP three times successfully attacked German and Norwegian ships.

The first success came to a group of six Kittyhawk fighter-bombers of the 78th IAP (leader – Captain V.P. Strelnikov) under the cover of six Airacobras of the 2nd GKAP (leader – Guards Captain D.P. Maksimovich) which flew a 'free-hunting' mission in Varanger Fjord. From the report of Captain P.P. Strelnikov:

> Take-off at 8:55, Rosta – Ura-Guba – Korabelny – Vaitolahti – Kibergnes Cape to the south along the coast to the west of Vadsø. Low-altitude flight to Kibergnes, further flight at 500m. At 9:45, near Andersby Cape, we attacked a group of eight to nine motorboats, including two patrol boats. After our strike, the remaining motorboats were attacked with machine-gun and cannon fire from Airacobra aircraft and one motorboat was sunk as a result. As a result of the strike, I observed a direct hit [by bombs – Author's note] on a cluster of motorboats. Two motorboats remained afloat after the strike. As a result of the strike, up to six motorboats were destroyed, including two patrol ships. On the return route, four enemy aircraft were seen flying out to intercept us, but they were too late. There was no combat with enemy aircraft.

As a result of the attack, Northern Fleet Air Force Headquarters credited five sunken motorboats to the pilots of the 78th IAP, while the Airacobra escort pilots were credited one motorboat. According to the German records, fishing motorboats were attacked, three of which were sunk.

Five Kittyhawks of the 78th IAP (leader – Major V.I. Babernov) were the next to achieve success. From the report of Senior Lieutenant A.I. Batrakov:

> I was a wingman in the second pair of four Kittyhawks. We took off at 9:00 following the route Rosta – Tsyp-Navolok – off-shore Vaitolahti – off-shore Vardö – Nolites Cape – target. At 10:00, I attacked a self-propelled barge east of Chelneset Cape. The bombs of the other two aircraft were dropped with 50–100m undershoot. I saw my own bombs explode three to five metres from the stern. After the explosion, the barge changed course by 90 degrees. After the bombing, I made three runs firing machine guns. The barge stopped moving. All aircraft of the group made a strike on the barge with machine-gun fire.

It should be noted that other pilots confirmed that it was Senior Lieutenant A.I. Batrakov's bomb that was the only one to explode close to the target. German documents state: "From 09:58 till 10:11, in Kongs Fjord, four Il-2s attacked the motor ship *Henriette of the Speer* of the Transport Flotilla with bombs and cannon/machine-gun fire. Two Norwegians were wounded and the ship was towed to Berlevåg by a Luftwaffe sea rescue boat."

The third attack on the German ships was again carried out by Captain V.P. Strelnikov. A group of eight Kittyhawks of the 78th IAP led by him, under the cover of eight Airacobras of the 2nd GKAP flew on a 'free-hunting' mission in the Varanger Fjord. From the report of Captain V.P. Strelnikov:

> Take-off at 15:05, Rosta – Ura-Guba – Korabelniy – Vaitolahti – Eckerö – Jacobselv. Flight altitude from low to 500m. At 16:00, the group attacked a cluster of small boats in the port of Jacobselv. As a result of the attack, I observed a direct hit of 11 FAB-100s in the cluster of small boats, after the hit I observed sinking of three barges of a displacement up to 300 tonnes, two motorboats, and one tug of 200–250 tonnes. Senior Lieutenant Mitrofanov destroyed a stone structure near the pier.

From the German documents it is known that as a result of the attack one tugboat, three motorboats, one amphibious assault boat were sunk, and two similar boats were damaged, but managed to run aground. The report of Captain V.P. Strelnikov further states the following: "When retreating after the strike, south-west of Vadsø we met six Bf 109s and engaged in air combat. Seven to eight minutes later four more Bf 109s appeared from south-east. The air combat was carried out during a withdrawal to Vaitolahti. I observed one Bf 109 coming down 1.5km west of Eckerö".

From the report of the Commander of the 6th IAD:

> The Airacobra aircraft fulfilled the task of escorting the Kittyhawks well. On the return route from Eckerö to Pummanki our aircraft were engaged in an air combat against 10 Bf 109s and six FW 190s, which resulted in the shooting down of two FW 190s and one Bf 109. Two Airacobras and two pilots were lost.

The Northern Fleet Air Force Headquarters credited one downed Bf 109 to Guards Captain N.M. Didenko and one downed FW 190 to Lieutenant Major V.I. Mukhin and Lieutenant A.F. Belyaev of the 2nd GKAP each. Two Airacobras of the 2nd GKAP piloted by Guards Lieutenant N.Ya. Markov and Guards Lieutenant N.M. Volkov did not return from the mission. According to research by Eric Mombeek, at the same time Bf 109s and FW 190s of the *Stab* IV./JG, as well as 14. and 15. *Staffeln* of the JG 5 were fighting against the Soviet aircraft. The Luftwaffe pilots claimed three downed Soviet aircraft losing one of their fighters; its pilot bailed out.

30 September

A group of four Kittyhawk fighter-bombers of the 78th IAP (leader – Senior Lieutenant V.G. Mitrofanov) under the cover of four Airacobras of the 2nd GKAP successfully attacked German landing ships. From the report of Senior Lieutenant V.G. Mitrofanov:

> Take-off at 6:35, following along the route Rosta – Ura-Guba – Korabelny – Vaitolahti – north of Eckerö – Jacobselv. Flight altitude from low to 600m. A barge and two motorboats were attacked at Jacobselv at 7:30. My bombs hit the barge directly. The barge sank. The barge has a displacement of about 600 tonnes. The bombs of Dzyuba and Baev fell two to three metres away from the motorboats. The motorboat sank [one victory was credited to two pilots – *Author's note*].

According to German documents: "07:40–07:45, 19 aircraft, one motorboat severely damaged, two lightly". Unlike the previous day, this group of fighter-bombers had no encounters with Luftwaffe aircraft.

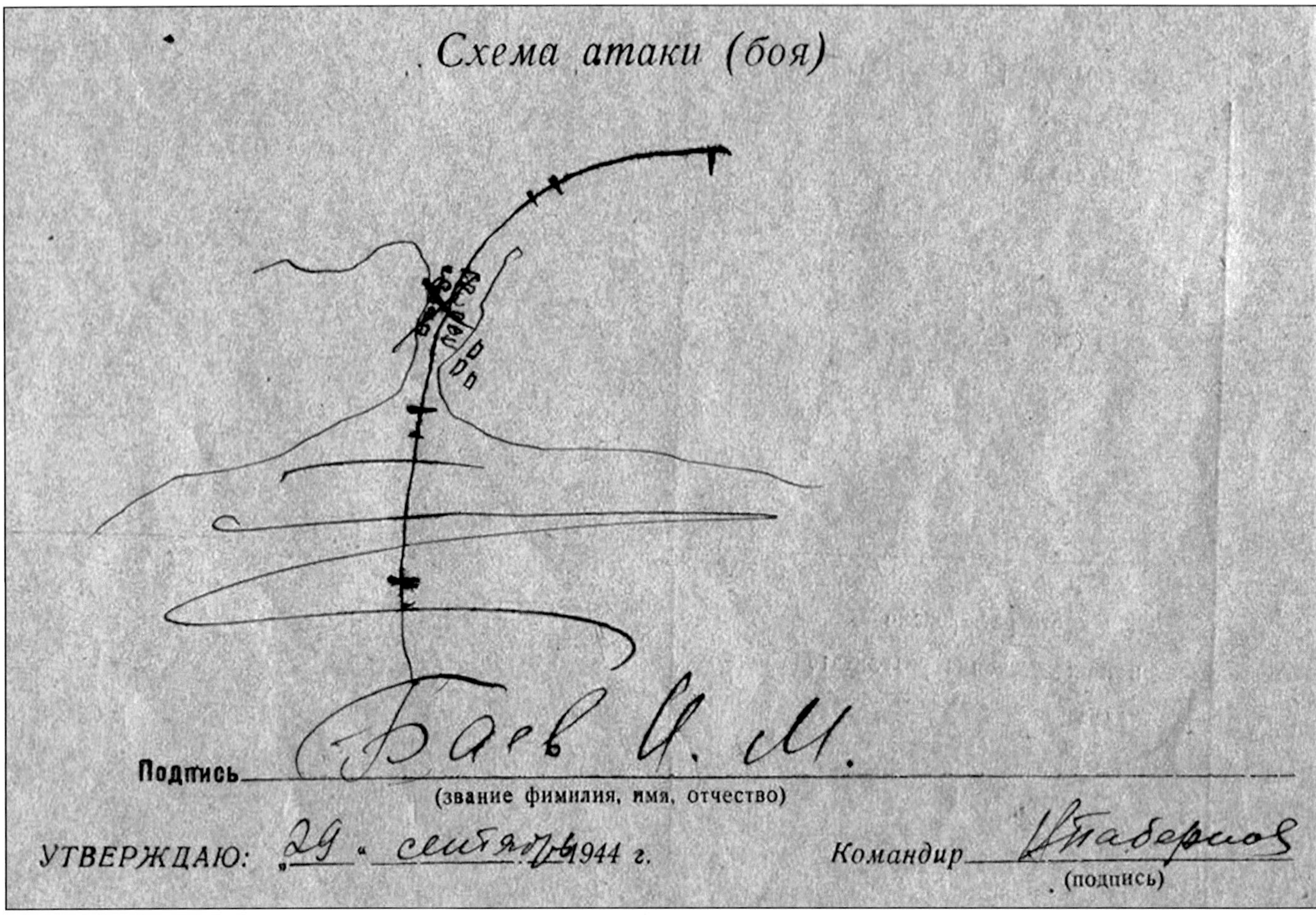

Plan of attack on German small boats by Kittyhawks of the 78th IAP near Jacobselv on 29 September 1944.

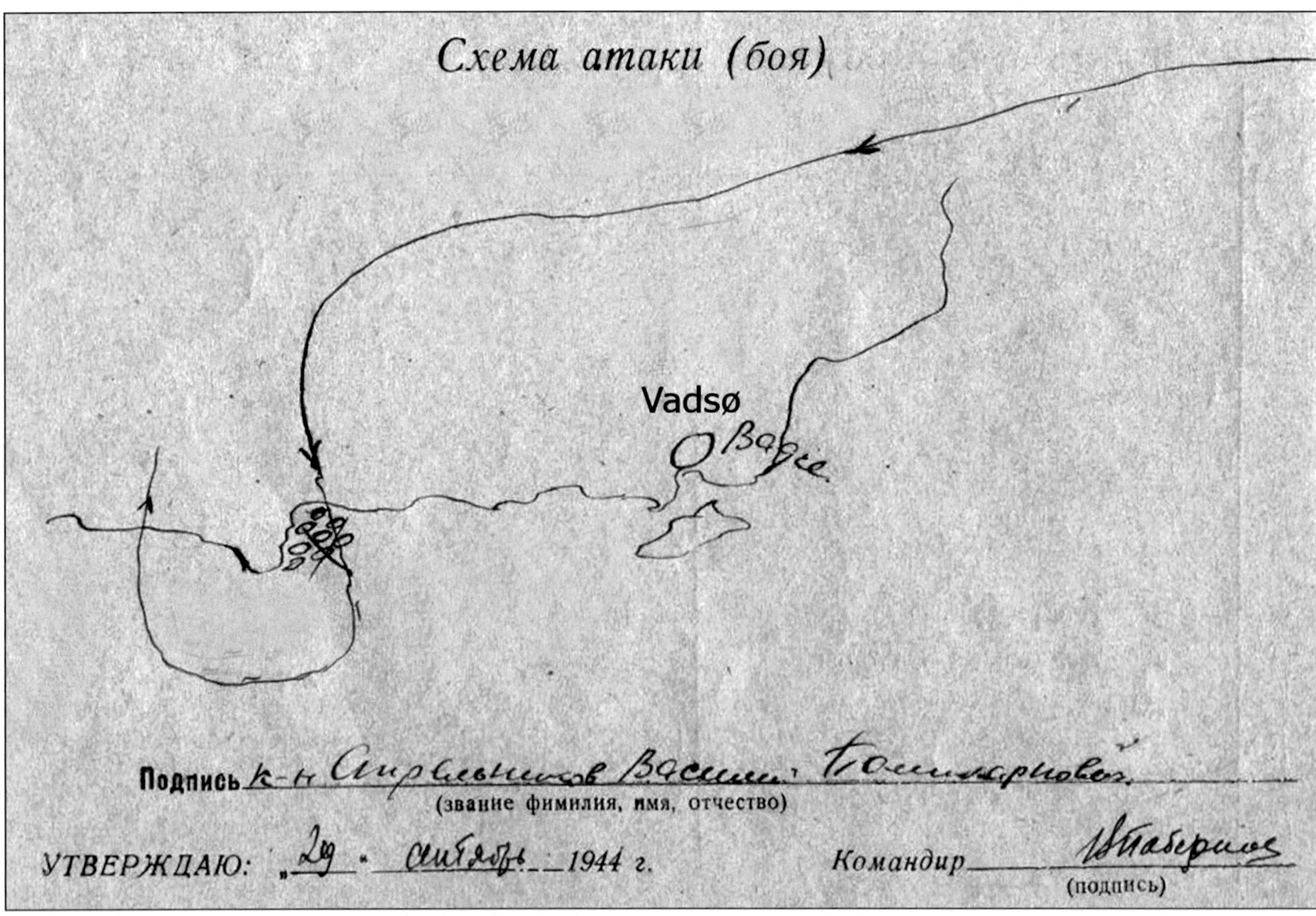

Plan of attack on German motorboats by Kittyhawks of the 78th IAP near Andersby on 29 September 1944.

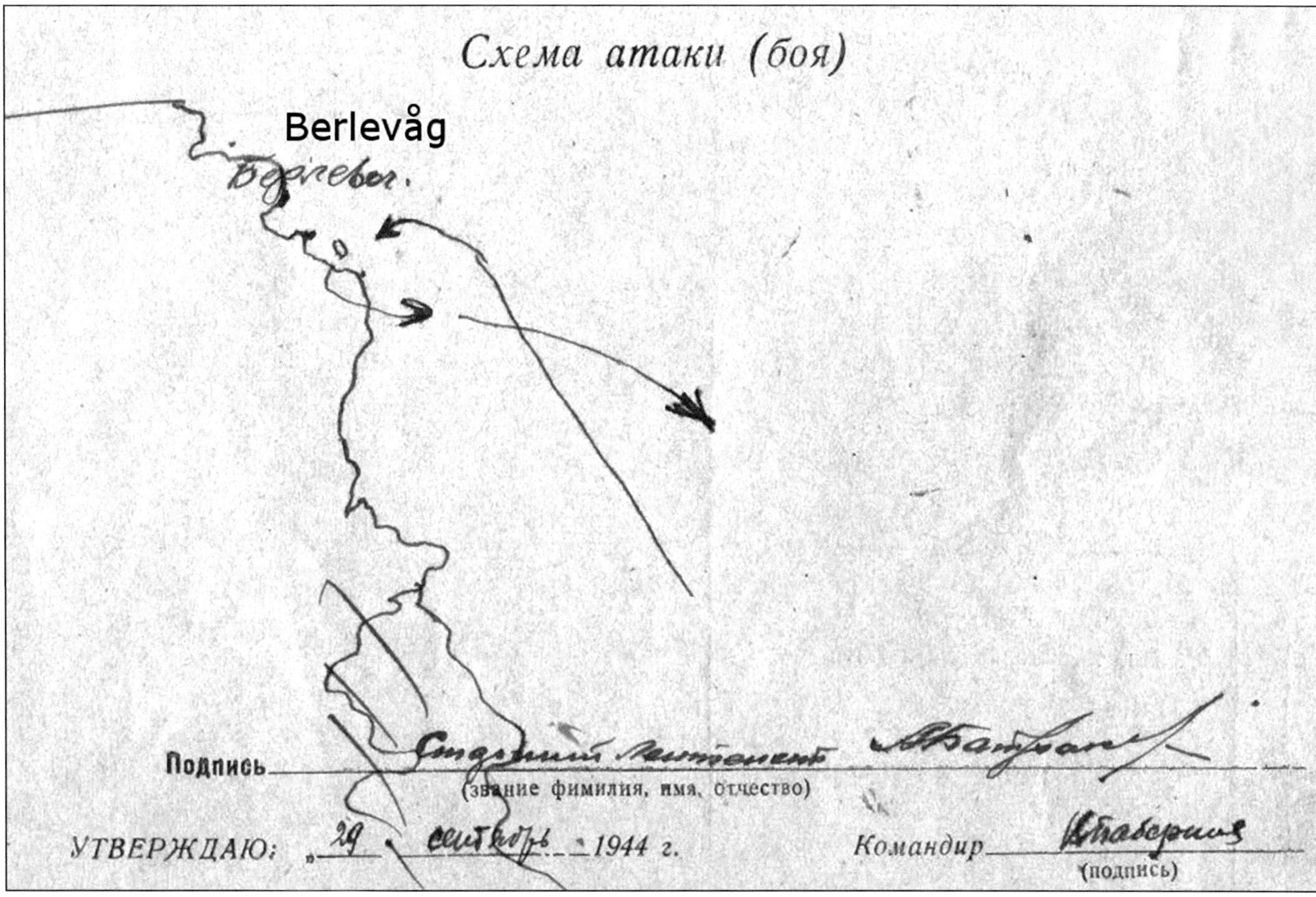

Plan of attack on motor ship *Henriette of the Speer* by Kittyhawks of the 78th IAP (leader – Major V.I. Babernov) on 29 September 1944.

Photo reconnaissance report of the results of the air strike on German motorboats by Kittyhawks of the 78th IAP (leader – Captain V.P. Strelnikov) near Andersby on 29 September 1944.

УДАР группы "КИТТИХАУК" 78 АП по мелк.судэм.Р-н ЯКОБСЭЛЬВЕН.

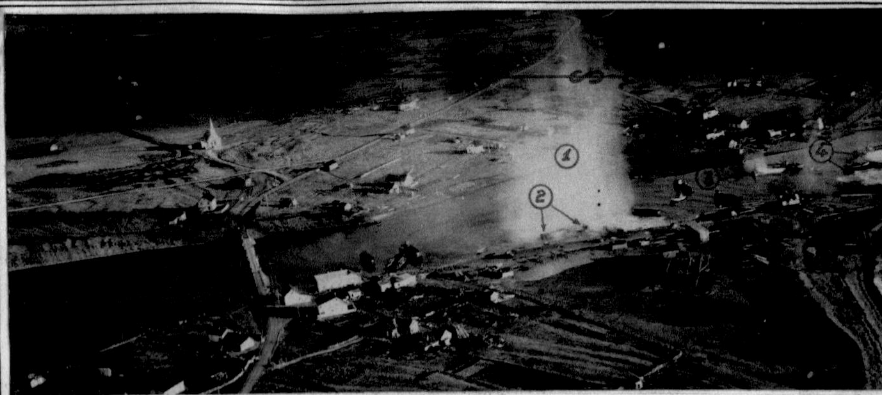

Фотодонесение:	Результэты дешифрировэния:
78 ИАП. БОЖКО. АФА-ИМ. Н=500 м. 16.00 29.09.44г. С-т "Киттихэук"	1. Серия рэзр.бомб. 2.Бэржэ и м/бот под рэзр. бомб. 3.Рэзр.бомбы у м/ботэ. 4.Рэзр.бомб в непосредственной близости от мелких судов. 5.Нэ месте первых серийных рэзр.бомб бэржэ с диферентом нэ корму и один м/бот с креном нэ корму. 6.Рэзр.бомб. 7.М/бот под рэзр.бомб. 8.Пулеметнэя очередь. 9.Один м/бот тонет. 10-11. Тонет один м/бот и рядом обломки от зэтонувших судов.

Photo reconnaissance report of the results of the air strike on German small boats by Kittyhawks of the 78th IAP near Jacobselv on 29 September 1944.
<u>Photo reconnaissance reporting</u>
78th IAP, pilot Bozhko; AFA-IM camera; Altitude 500m; 16:00, 29 September 1944; Kittyhawk aircraft.
<u>Results of the photo reconnaissance interpretation</u>
1. Series of bomb explosions.
2. Barge and motorboat under the bomb explosions.
3. Bomb explosions near the motorboat.
4. Bomb explosions in the close proxwimity to small boats.
5. At the location of the first series of bomb explosions – a barge with the stern trim and one motor boat listing to the stern.
6. Bomb explosions.
7. A motorboat under the bomb explosions.
8. Machine-gun fire.
9. One motorboat sinking.
10. One motorboat sinking, and fragments of sunk ships nearby.

БОМБО-УДАР ГРУППЫ "КИТТИХАУК" 78 АП

ПО МЕЛКИМ СУДАМ ПР-КА В РАЙОНЕ сел. ЯКОБСЭЛЬВЕН7

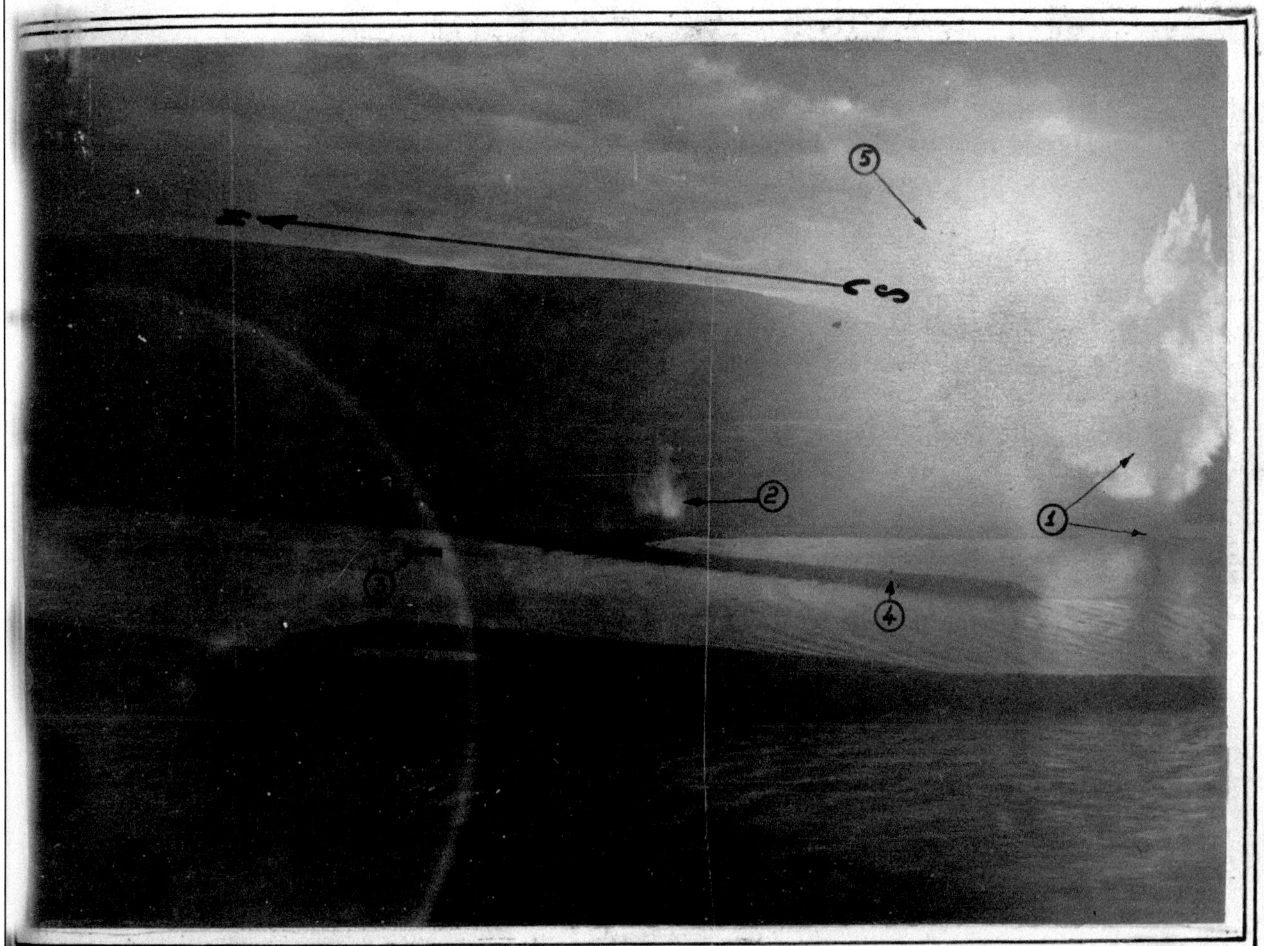

ФОТОДОНЕСЕНИЕ:

78 ИАП.

Л-к Б Р А Й К О.

АФА-ИМ Н=200 м.

07.30 30.09.44 г.

С-т "Киттихаук".

РЕЗУЛЬТАТЫ ДЕШИФРИРОВАНИЯ:

1. Взрыв нефтеналивного судна, столб дыма и воды достигает двух сот метров.
2. Разрывы авиабомб в районе жилых помещений.
3. Один мотобот на рейде.
4. Каменный м о л.
5. Восход с о л н ц а .

Photo reconnaissance report of the results of the air strike on Jacobselv by Kittyhawks of the 78th IAP on 30 September 1944.

Photo reconnaissance reporting

78th IAP, pilot Braiko; AFA-IM camera; Altitude 200m; 07:30, 30 September 1944; Kittyhawk aircraft.

Results of the photo reconnaissance interpretation

1. Explosion of the oil tanker. The column of smoke and water reaches an altitude of 200m.
2. Bomb explosions in the area of apartment houses.
3. One motorboat.
4. Stone mole.
5. Sunrise.

4
KITTYHAWKS, OCTOBER 1944

October 1944 was the last and probably the most successful month for the 78th IAP. During that month the regiment pilots were able to deliver precise strikes against both coastal shipping and German ships. During the Petsamo-Kirkenes offensive that had begun, the Kittyhawks struck ground targets and were even used as transport aircraft.

On 1 October 1944, the 78th IAP had on its strength 31 serviceable and six unserviceable Kittyhawks. In addition, the regiment had one serviceable and one unserviceable training Kittyhawks with dual control and one serviceable Po-2 trainer.

The main airfield of the regiment was Rosta, where 20 serviceable and three unserviceable Kittyhawks were based. The Pummanki airfield accommodated 11 serviceable and three unserviceable Kittyhawks. All training aircraft were stationed at the Rosta airfield.

The staff of the 78th IAP numbered 41 pilots, five engineers, 70 technicians and mechanics, 77 lower ranks, 22 support staff (medics, personnel of the canteen, etc.). The total number was 215 men.

During October 1944, the 78th IAP made 487 combat flights, 150 of which were targeted against ships and convoys. Nearly the same number of missions, 147, was flown against ground targets, mostly German troops, and another 47 against enemy bases. In the course of combat operations, the pilots of the regiment shot down six Bf 109s, one FW 190, one Ju 88 and a BV 138 flying boat. Their own aircraft losses amounted six Kittyhawks, all from enemy action. Two pilots of the regiment did not return from combat missions.

The reconnaissance aircraft of the 118th RAP succeeded in performing a large number of missions in October 1944. On 1 October, the regiment had 36 combat aircraft, nine of which were Kittyhawks. Unfortunately, one reconnaissance Kittyhawk did not return from a combat flight on 15 October. It was the second combat loss of the 118th RAP in the entire period of operating this aircraft type.

10 October

At 13:50, five Kittyhawk fighter-bombers and one reconnaissance Kittyhawk of the 78th IAP (leader – Captain V.P. Strelnikov), covered by four Airacobras of the 2nd GKAP flew to Berlevåg for a 'free hunting' mission. At 14:40, the Kittyhawks found a target. From the combat flight log of 6th IAD:

> In the area of Syulte Fjord at Korenes Cape, the aircraft attacked one patrol motorboat of up to 130 tonnes displacement using the skip-bombing method with simultaneous machine-gun fire. As a result of direct hits from three FAB-100s, the patrol motorboats sank.

According to German data, the bombs hit the Norwegian motorboat *Boelgen*. Three Norwegians and two Germans were killed. The Northern Fleet Air Force Headquarters credited sinking of the motorboat to Lieutenant I.M. Baev.

11 October

As the day before, the fighter-bombers of the 78th IAP were engaged in the usual activity of disrupting coastal shipping.

At 8:35, six Kittyhawks of the 78th IAP (leader – Captain V.P. Strelnikov) took off with the task of destroying small ships and boats from Vardö to Kongs Fjord. From the report of Captain V.P. Strelnikov:

> Our search for a target from Vardö to Kongs Fjord didn't result in detecting any enemy ships. The decision was made to cross the coast at Kongs Fjord and fly towards the coast at Vardö; when approaching the southern part of Bos Fjord we spotted clusters of small ships and boats. I decided to attack.

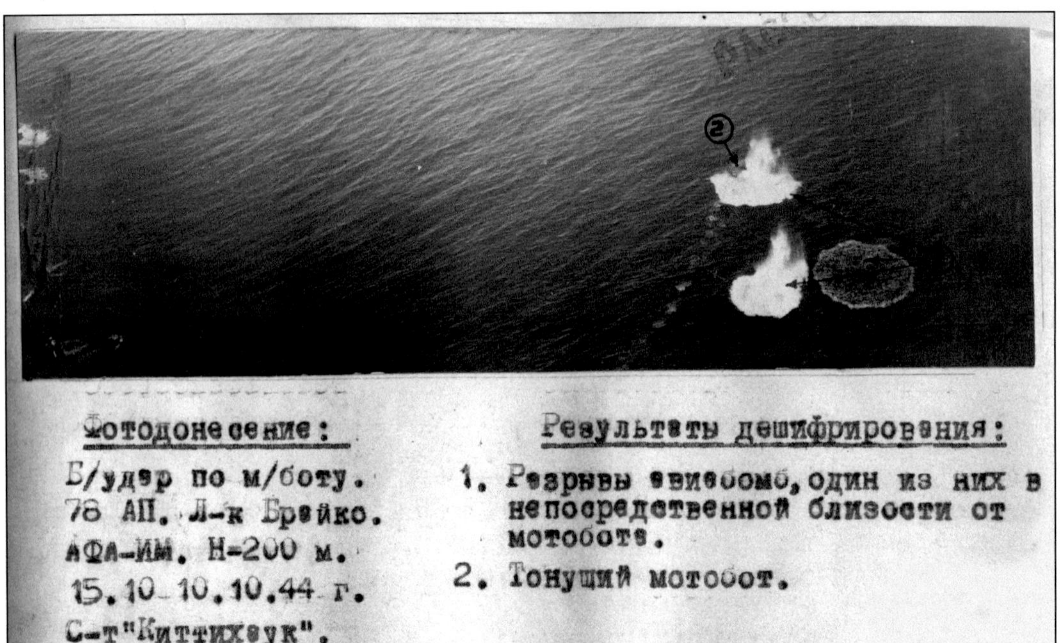

Photo reconnaissance report of the results of the air strike by Kittyhawks of the 78th IAP on 10 October 1944.
Photo reconnaissance reporting
Bomb strike on a motorboat; 78th IAP, pilot Braiko; AFA-IM camera; Altitude 200m; 15:10, 10 October 1944; Kittyhawk aircraft.
Results of the photo reconnaissance interpretation
1. Bomb explosions, one of them in the close proximity to the motorboat.
2. Motorboat sinking.

From the combat flight log of the 6th IAD:

> At 09:30, the aircraft conducted a strike using the skip-bombing method from an altitude of 25–20m and from a distance of 120–100m against the reserve target of 25 motorboats and enemy barges in the Bos Fjord area and fired machine guns at them. As a result of the strike, four motorboats and one self-propelled 400-tonne barge were sunk. Machine-gun fire set fire to one motorboat, one light anti-aircraft artillery gun was suppressed.

According to German documents, after the air strike the pier caught fire, and the motorboat and small boat sank. The success was somewhat spoilt by the fact that the German anti-aircraft artillery was able to target well and shoot down the photo reconnaissance Kittyhawk piloted by Lieutenant V.S. Bozhko. The report on the loss of the aircraft states: "While photographing the results of the strike, the aircraft was hit by light anti-aircraft artillery fire. The aircraft engine failed in the Polyarny area. The pilot ditched the aircraft in the Kola Bay. The aircraft sank; the pilot was picked up by motorboats." Another aircraft damaged by the German anti-aircraft artillery was the Kittyhawk of Captain V.P. Strelnikov, which, having been hit in the wing by a 20mm shell, reached the airfield without any problems.

Four hours later, the group led by Captain V.P. Strelnikov attacked the German motorboats in Bos Fjord again. At 12:45, six Kittyhawks of the 78th IAP took off from the Rosta airfield. One hour later they reached Bos Fjord. From the combat flight log of the 6th IAD:

> At 13:37, from an altitude of 25–30m and distance of 150–120m, the aircraft conducted a strike using a skip-bombing method on 10–12 enemy motorboats and barges in Bos Fjord and fired machine guns at them. As a result of the strike, two motorboats and one barge of 500–600 tonnes displacement (presumably with ammunition) were sunk, the pier was destroyed, the ammunition warehouse exploded, one light anti-aircraft artillery gun was suppressed.

According to German data, several German motor ships were lightly damaged during the attack. In contrast to the morning mission, the anti-aircraft fire in the afternoon was completely ineffective, and all Kittyhawks safely returned to their airfield.

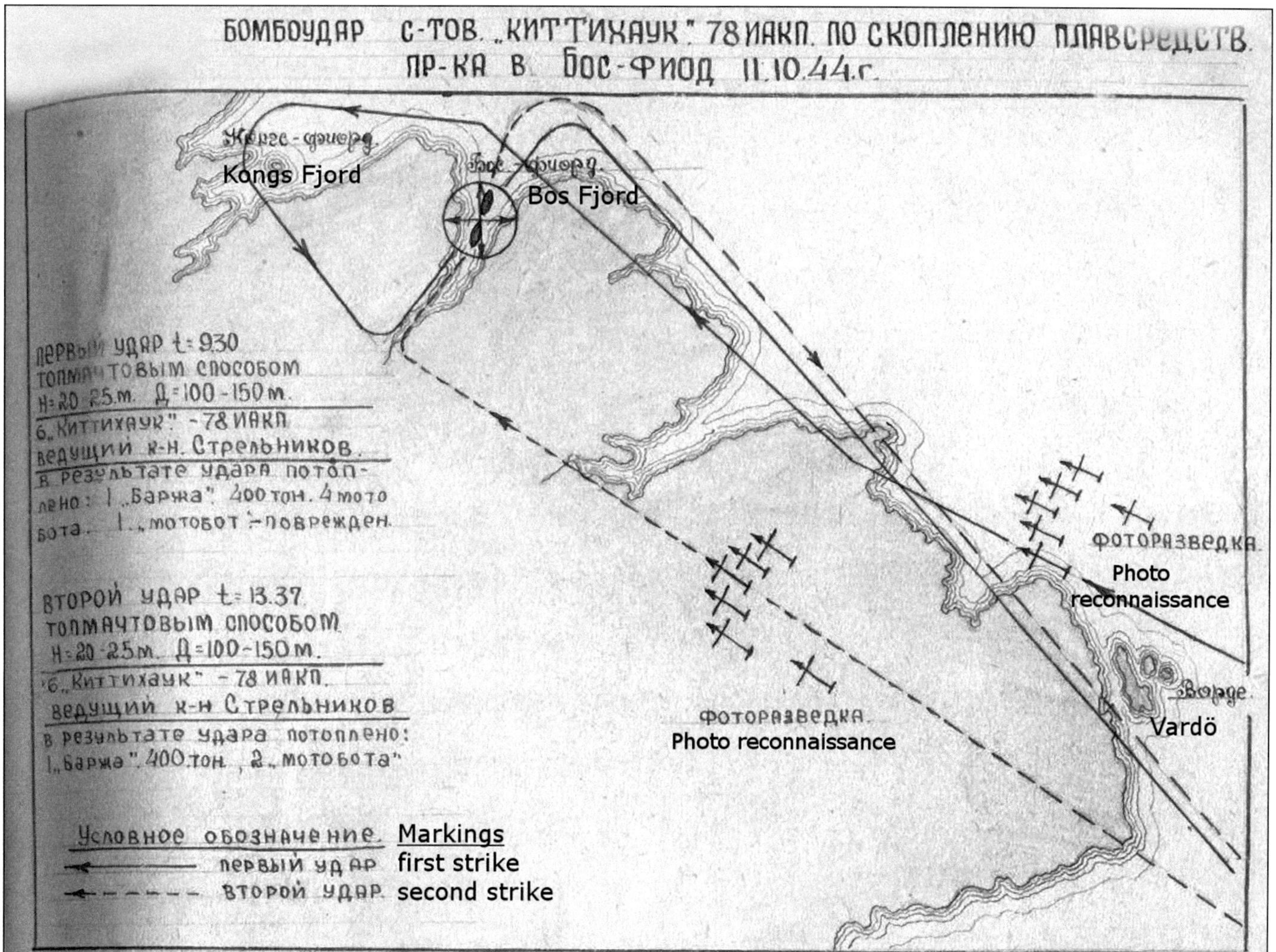

Plan of attack by aircraft of the 78th IAP on 11 October 1944.
<u>First strike</u>
Time 9:30; Skip-bombing method; Altitude 20–25m; distance 100–150m; Six Kittyhawks of the 78th IAP; Leader – Captain Strelnikov; As the result of the strike: – one barge (400grt) and four motorboats were sunk; – one motorboat damaged.
<u>Second strike</u>
Time 13:37; Skip-bombing method; Altitude 20–25m; distance 100–150m; Six Kittyhawks of the 78th IAP; Leader – Captain Strelnikov; As the result of the strike: – one barge (400grt) and two motorboats were sunk.

Команд. 1 аэ 78 иап
(Должность, часть)
капитан Стрельников В.П.
(Звание, фамилия, имя, отчество)
« 11 » октября 1944 г.

3

Командиру 78 иап
майору Бабуркову
(Звание, фамилия)

РАПОРТ

О выполнении боевого полета «свободная охота» на коммуникациях противника

№№ п/п	ВОПРОСЫ	ОТВЕТЫ
1.	В составе какой группы вылетал на задание	6 истребителей на свободную охоту от Варде на запад до Кунгс-фиорд
2.	Время взлета, маршрут и профиль полета	взлет 8.35 Роста – [illegible] наволок – Цып-наволок – Вайталахта – Севернее Варде 10-15 км – Кунгс фиорд Н = бреющая – 400 м.
3.	Что атаковано, время и место атаки (боя)	в 9.30 в Бос-фиорде у причалов атаковали скопление мелких плав. средств мотоботы, баржи, буксиры до 25 штук
4.	Наблюдения о действиях других самолетов—групп	—
5.	Наблюдение результатов Удары: а) своих б) соседей	наблюдал попадание своих бомб в мотоботы, попадание бомб в мотобот ст. л-та Митрофанов попадание бомб мл. л-та Гуцева в баржу 400 тонн, попадание бомб Дзюбы в один мотобот, мл. л-та Баева в скопление мотоботов мл. л-ты Баев и Гуцев подавили огнем пулеметов МЗА пр-ка После бомбометания произвели штурмовку в результате подожгли еще один мотобот.
6.	Что сфотографировано в подтверждение результатов удара	результат фотографировался мл. л-том Божко с-т которого был подбит ЗА в результате чего произвел вынужденную посадку на воду около Полярного с-т затонул летчик подобран.

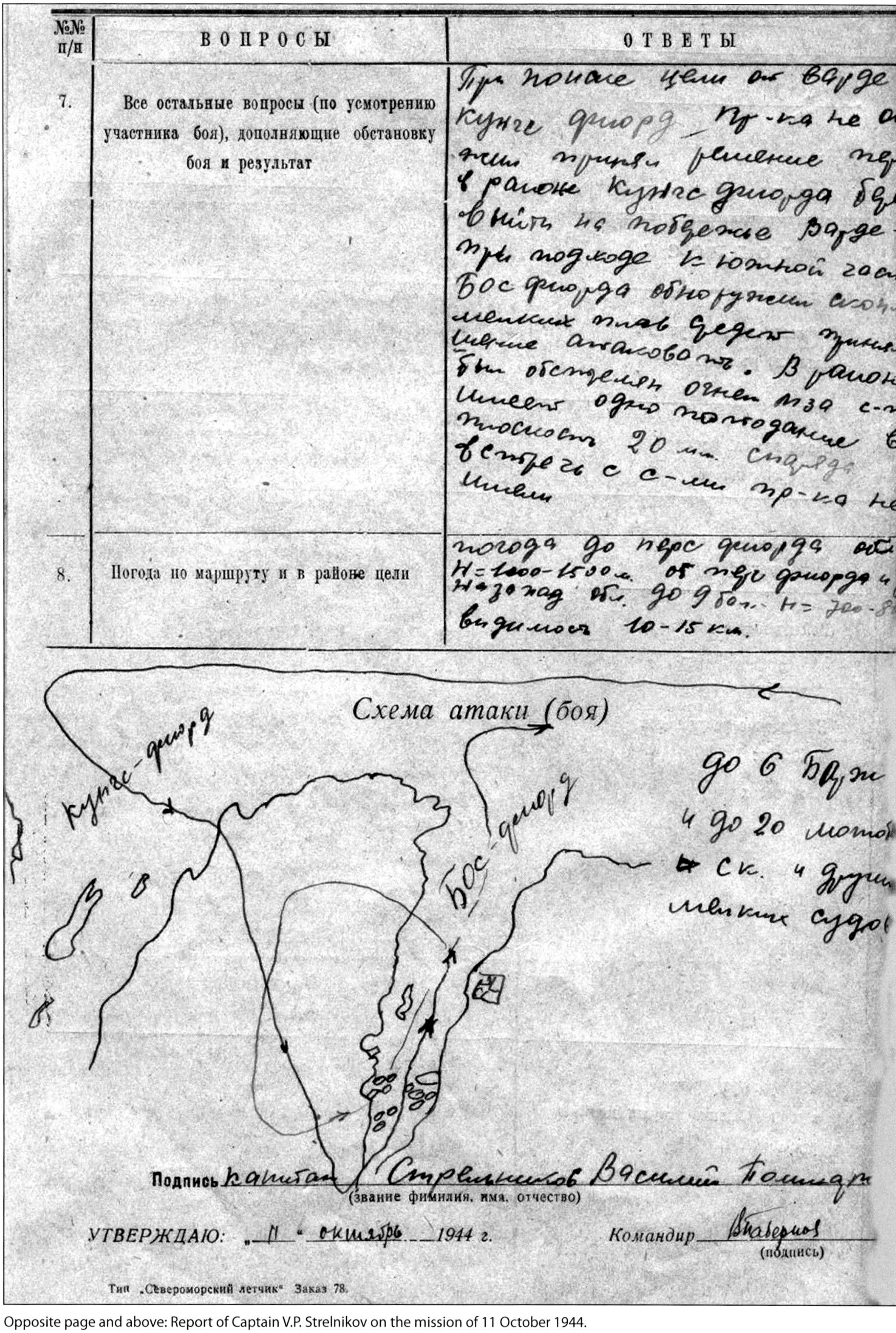

№№ п/п	ВОПРОСЫ	ОТВЕТЫ
7.	Все остальные вопросы (по усмотрению участника боя), дополняющие обстановку боя и результат	При поиске цели от Варде Кунгс фиорд пр-ка не об[illegible] принял решение [illegible] в районе Кунгс фиорда [illegible] выйти на побережье Варде. При подходе к южной части Бос фиорда обнаружил скопление мелких плав средств [illegible] атаковать. [illegible] был обстрелян. В районе имеет одно попадание в плоскость 20 мм снаряда [illegible] с-ми пр-ка не [illegible]
8.	Погода по маршруту и в районе цели	погода до Бос фиорда обл. Н=1000-1500 м. от Бос фиорда и на запад обл. до 9 бал. Н=700-8[illegible] видимость 10-15 км.

Подпись капитан Стрельников Василий [illegible]
(звание фимилия, имя, отчество)

УТВЕРЖДАЮ: „11" октября 1944 г. Командир [signature]
(подпись)

Тип „Североморский летчик" Заказ 78.

Opposite page and above: Report of Captain V.P. Strelnikov on the mission of 11 October 1944.

12 October

In the evening of 11 October 1944, the first convoy with evacuated equipment and personnel set out from Kirkenes. The convoy Ki.135.Lf included minesweepers M-31, M-35, M-251, patrol ships V-6107, V-6110, V-6114, UJ-1219, UJ-1220, motor minesweeper R-156, barge/floating workshop D-152-P, steamers *Krükau* (493grt), *Lumme* (1,730grt), *Pommern* (198grt) and *Egerland* (212grt).

Around 6:40 on 12 October 1944, near Pers Fjord the convoy was spotted by a reconnaissance Kittyhawk of the 118th RAP.

At 10:00, eight Il-2s of the 46th ShAP (leader – Senior Lieutenant N.N. Surovov) covered by eight Yak-7Bs of the 20th IAP (leader – Senior Lieutenant K.V. Boychenko) and four Kittyhawks of the 78th IAP performed a dive attack on the convoy at Makkaur Cape. The patrol ships V-6110 and V-6114 were lightly damaged by the cannon and machine-gun fire of the attackers. Four crewmembers were killed and six were wounded.

There were no Luftwaffe fighters over the convoy, so the escort fighters attacked the German anti-submarine seaplanes. From the report of Junior Lieutenant L.I. Pustobaev, a pilot of Kittyhawk of the 78th IAP:

> Senior Lieutenant Nikolayev attacked a BV 138 in the convoy area at 10:02, at 10:04 he shot down the aircraft on the eastern side of Kongs Fjord, it fell into the water burning. I observed the fall of another BV 138 which exploded after the attack of Lieutenant Demidov.

Based on the results of the air combat the Northern Fleet Air Fleet Headquarters credited one downed BV 138 each to Lieutenant E.Z. Demidov of the 20th IAP and to Lieutenant A.F. Nikolayev of the 78th IAP.

After the attack on the convoy, the Soviet aircraft were intercepted by Luftwaffe fighters; in the course of the air combat two Yak-7Bs of the 20th IAP were shot down. The pilot of one Yak-7B, Junior Lieutenant V.V. Buslaev, was killed, and the second, Lieutenant E.I. Gorobets, was picked up by a Catalina rescue seaplane of the 118th RAP. This was the first and, apparently, the only case in which a Northern Fleet Air Force rescue aircraft was able to save the pilot of a downed aircraft.

The Northern Fleet Air Force Headquarters credited the only victory over the FW 190 in the air combat to the Il-2 gunner of the 46th ShAP, Sergeant V.S. Uvarov.

It is possible that Luftwaffe fighters of the 13./JG 5 participated in this combat. The German pilots claimed to have shot down one Soviet aircraft, losing one of their own.

While one group of Kittyhawks was escorting attack aircraft to strike the convoy, the other was hunting for the enemy ships. Six Kittyhawk fighter-bombers of the 78th IAP (leader – Captain V.P. Strelnikov) flew out for a 'free hunting' mission. At 13:35, they attacked, according to pilots' reports, motorboats and barges at Jacobselv. The pilots reported sinking of two barges and three motorboats. According to Norwegian reports, fishing boats were hit and several Norwegians were wounded.

Photo reconnaissance report of the results of the air strike by Kittyhawks of the 78th IAP on 12 October 1944.
Photo reconnaissance reporting
Bomb strike on small boats; 78th IAP, pilot Braiko; AFA-IM camera; Altitude 200m; 13:35, 12 October 1944; Kittyhawk aircraft
Results of the photo reconnaissance interpretation
1. In the bomb explosions, one motorboat listing to port.
2. Barge sinking.
3. Bomb explosions in the area of small boats concentration.
4. Motorboat sinking.

15 October

The Kittyhawks continued to hunt small vessels – a pair of Kittyhawks of the 78th IAP (leader – Senior Lieutenant A.F. Nikolayev) flew out for a 'free hunting' mission. From the report of Senior Lieutenant A.F. Nikolayev:

> The aircraft took off at 8:30 and followed the route Heinesaari – Eckerö – 10km west of Vadsø, flying at a low altitude. At 8:55, 10km west of Eckerö we attacked one high-speed landing barge using the skip-bombing method. We observed a direct hit of one FAB-100 in the bow of the barge, the barge caught fire, the other FAB-100 did not detach, then we made two attack approaches. The barge sank. During the next mission we observed an oil slick in the area of attack.

According to German documents, two aircraft bombed and fired machine-guns at the motorboat, which was carrying cargo for the German army. As a result of the attack, the vessel sustained damage.

At 10:45, a reconnaissance Kittyhawk of the 118th RAP piloted by Junior Lieutenant P.I. Ovchinnikov took off from Pummanki airfield to reconnoitre a front-line road between Liinahamari and Kirkenes. The aircraft did not return at the estimated time. There is information on military-historical forums that the aircraft crashed near the Luostari airfield and the remains of the pilot were buried by a search party.

16 October

A group of four Kittyhawk fighter-bombers of the 78th IAP (leader – Senior Lieutenant A.F. Nikolayev) achieved another success during a 'free-hunting' mission.

According to the pilots' report, at 8:07, the aircraft struck two self-propelled barges in the Kobbholm Fjord using skip-bombing method. Probably their target was the high-speed landing barge AF-24, which reported the Soviet aircraft attacks. However, two hours later, at 10:15, the same group attacked 'speedboats', as reported by the pilots. According to German documents, patrol boats V-6703, V-6706, V-6713 were hit. A bomb hit the V-6706.[2] The ship caught fire, ran aground and was completely burnt out by the end of the day. Two of the ship's crew were killed and three injured.

Most interestingly, the Northern Fleet Air Force Headquarters considered the attack unsuccessful.

17 October

In the morning, a pair of Kittyhawks of the 78th IAP (leader – Lieutenant D.P. Dzyuba) searched for pilots who had not returned from the missions of the previous days. Unfortunately, the Soviet pilots were not found, while the Germans were forced to look for their own crews. Lieutenant D.P. Dzyuba spotted a solitary Ju 88 near Vardö. From the combat flight log of 6th IAD: "At 9:15, a Ju 88 was spotted and attacked near Komagver. Lieutenant Dzyuba shot down one Ju 88". The Northern Fleet Air Force Headquarters credited the victory over the Ju 88 to Lieutenant D.P. Dzyuba. According to German documents, on this day a Ju 88D-1/Tr, W.Nr. 430571, aircraft code 'G2+NH', of the 1.*(F)/Aufklärungsgruppe* 124 was shot down. The crew, led by the squadron commander, *Hptm.* Reinhold Wünsche, were posted missing. It should be noted that Luftwaffe pilots attempted to find the missing reconnaissance aircraft. The search resulted in another lost Ju 88D, although it was shot down by German anti-aircraft artillery.

Meanwhile, a reconnaissance Kittyhawk of the 118th RAP spotted another convoy. It was Lf.138.Ki that left Lo Fjord on 16 October 1944. At 8:00, the Kittyhawk spotted it near Svartnes Cape. The convoy consisted of gunboat K-3, patrol ship V-6107, submarine hunter UJ-1219, minesweepers M-302, M-321, M-322, M-382, motor minesweepers R-57, R-121, R-302, floating base of the motor minesweepers *Paris* (1,753grt), steamer *Adamsturm* (1,923grt), and tanker *Adlergrund* (698grt).

At 9:00, attack aircraft took off from Pummanki to strike the convoy. At 9:40, two groups of six Il-2s each of the 46th ShAP (leaders – Senior Lieutenants V.M. Skopintsev and N.N. Surovov), covered by 12 Yak-7Bs of the 20th IAP and four Kittyhawks of the 78th IAP, attacked the convoy near Eckerö Cape. The attack resulted in the sinking of the patrol ship V-6107.

However, the Soviet aircraft were attacked over the target by a large group of Luftwaffe fighters and lost five aircraft along with their crews. The divisional report for the fourth quarter of the 14th SAD states that Senior Lieutenant V.I. Skopintsev was to blame for the losses of the attack aircraft. The division commander accused the leader of the group of Il-2s of attacking through the clouds alone, without the cover of his fighters, and that the fighters covering his group were not informed of the manoeuvre. The Luftwaffe fighters were under the clouds and were virtually invisible before they attacked the Soviet aircraft.

The Kittyhawks, which were covering the Il-2s, came to their aid and engaged in air combat. From the combat flight log of the 6th IAD: "There was an air combat against a group of up to 20 Bf 109s and FW 190s over the convoy. As a result, Lieutenant Molchanov shot down one Bf 109. The aircraft went down near Eckerö".

On the German side, the fighters from the *Stab* III./JG 5, and 9., 10. and 13. *Staffeln* of the JG 5 participated in the air combat. The Luftwaffe pilots claimed about 10 downed Soviet aircraft, losing one Bf 109 of 10./JG 5. Its pilot, *Unteroffizier* Karl-Heinz Fuchs, was killed. According to the book by Eric Mombeek, the Bf 109 of *Leutnant* W. Heinicke of the 9. *Staffel* was also hit, but the pilot managed to reach Kirkenes airfield. The aircraft was damaged beyond repair. Another Bf 109 of the 10. *Staffel* was hit by Il-2 fire and made an emergency landing. Its pilot, *Feldwebel* D. Vollmann, survived.

The Northern Fleet Air Force Headquarters credited seven downed Luftwaffe fighters to the pilots and air gunners. Il-2 pilot Lieutenant V.I. Markovskiy, air gunners Sergeant V.S. Uvarov and Junior Sergeant P.I. Pyataev were credited one FW 190 each. One FW 190 was credited to two gunners: Sergeants N.I. Lidin and V.I. Gumenniy. Senior Lieutenant L.P. Lapin and Junior Lieutenant P.P. Starkov of the 20th IAP and the Kittyhawk pilot Lieutenant A.G. Molchanov of the 78th IAP were credited with one Bf 109 each.

21 October

The fifth evacuation convoy Ki.139.La left Kirkenes on 20 October 1944. The convoy consisted of patrol ships V-6308, V-6311, V-6312, Nki-06, minesweepers M-31, M-35, M-202, M-251, M-253, motor minesweepers R-121, R-160, R-202, R-301 steamers *Brigitte* (325grt), *Margaretha* (396grt), *Herma* (519grt), sailing ship *Moshulu* (3,520grt), and tugboats *Floyen II* (535grt), *Ostland* and *Jason* (296grt).

2 Historical note: the original designation of gunboat V-6706 was KFK-375. It was put into service in March 1944 and was part of the Kirkenes Harbour Patrol Flotilla under the name Nki-16. In May 1944, in connection with the patrol flotilla reforms, it was transferred to the 67th Patrol Boat Flotilla. It had a standard displacement of 110 tonnes. Length – 24m. The width – 6m. Draught – 2.75m. Armament: one 37mm cannon and one twin 20mm gun mount.

Despite numerous reconnaissance flights, the torpedo boats were the first to spot the convoy. On 21 October, at 1:30, the radar of the torpedo boat No. 230 detected the German convoy. About two o'clock in the morning the torpedo boats Nos. 230 and 205 launched a torpedo salvo against the convoy. As a result, motor minesweeper R-301 was hit by a torpedo. The torpedo did not explode, but the ship, which was badly damaged, had to return to Vardö, accompanied by two other motor minesweepers. Around four o'clock torpedo boats Nos. 215, 237 and 244 attacked the Germans. They launched torpedoes at the convoy and achieved one hit on the minesweeper M-31. This time the torpedo hit the centre of the hull and exploded. The minesweeper quickly sank, taking 56 sailors with it.

The critical situation of the motor minesweeper R-301, moving slowly towards Vardö, forced the German command to send tug *Jason* (296grt) and motor minesweepers R-151 and R-160 to its rescue. They became the first targets for the Kittyhawks that were on a 'free hunting' mission in the area of the Varanger Peninsula, from Makkaur to Eckerö Cape. From the report of Senior Lieutenant A.Ya. Shvailakh:

> Take-off at 7:46, Rosta – Pikshuev – Pummanki – Komagnes Cape – Svartnes – Pers Fjord. Flight altitude from 1,000 to 600m. At 8:35, the aircraft attacked a cargo-passenger vessel of 500–600 tonnes displacement at Pers Fjord, and a submarine hunter boat in the area offshore the Pers Fjord. My bombs, dropped by the skip-bombing method, hit the stern of the cargo-passenger vessel. I also fired machine guns at it. Bombs dropped by Lieutenant Seliverstov hit the middle of the side of the cargo-passenger vessel: the latter sank emitting smoke.

The tugboat *Jason* was struck by Senior Lieutenant A.Y. Shvailakh and Junior Lieutenant A.A. Seliverstov. From the combat log of the 1. *Küstensicherungsverband*: "At 06:42, the vessel sustained a heavy bomb hit, at 07:57 it was reported that attempts to extinguish the fire were futile, the ship was lost, finished off by artillery in 70.28.4 N. – 30.53.5 E". From the further text of the report of the Kittyhawks' leader: "The bombs of Lieutenant Skrebkov hit the side of the submarine hunter boat; the latter instantly disappeared under water. Lieutenant Kirillov dropped bombs [on the submarine hunter boat – *Author's note*] with undershoot".

From the report of the mechanical engineer of the Motor Minesweepers Flotilla:

> 06:32. R-151: while guarding the convoy, there was an attack by six Il-2s using bombs and machine-gun fire.[3] The first bomb exploded under the stern, and at the same time there were numerous holes from cannon and machine-gun fire on the starboard side in the engine room. The ship settled deep in the stern. Presumably, its compartments I and II were flooded. The engines continued to run at 'half throttle forward'. Following the impact of the first bomb, two more bombs exploded under the ship in the centre of the hull and the ship sustained further damage from cannon and machine-gun fire. The port engine and auxiliary engine immediately stopped, the electric generator and steering gear failed. The starboard engine continued to operate. At the same time there was a large inflow of water into compartments III and IV, the bulkhead between these compartments broke. Water was rising rapidly in the engine room. The water pumps could not cope with the situation. Due to the further rapid rise of water, the engine room personnel were ordered to abandon the engine room. The ship was slowly sinking aft. A little later, the starboard engine also stalled. The ship then sank rapidly by the stern. 06:45. R-151 sank. Presumably, the bombs exploded under the ship, rupturing the hull in compartments I to IV. Except for one sailor, who was lethally wounded by a shell, there were no more casualties among the crew members. The crew were evacuated by R-160.

Thus, the destruction of the motor minesweeper R-151 was credited to both pilots – Lieutenants N.N. Skrebkov and N.I. Kirillov.

While the Kittyhawks were hunting German ships and vessels, the command of the Northern Fleet Air Force decided to launch a massive strike against Kirkenes. The main objective was still to disrupt the organised evacuation of the Germans. Fifteen Bostons of the 36th MTAP, five Bostons of the 9th GMTAP, 17 Kittyhawks of the 78th IAP and 19 Il-2s of the 46th ShAP participated in this attack under the cover of fighters of the 2nd GKAP, 27th, 78th and 20th IAPs. All aircraft conducted the attack between 12:40 and 12:45.

At 12:40, 17 Kittyhawks of the 78th IAP (leader – Captain D.I. Sinev) dropped bombs on targets in Kirkenes. From the combat flight log of the 6th IAD:

> At 12:40, the aircraft dropped bombs from a dive, from an altitude of 1,200m, at the Kirkenes ore processing plant. The strike destroyed and burned down three warehouses in the area of the ore processing plant and the power plant; one house was set on fire.

Luftwaffe fighters attempted to attack Soviet aircraft in small groups. From the combat flight log of the 6th IAD:

> At 12:55, near Kirkenes, at 3,000m altitude, the aircraft were engaged in air combat against three Bf 109s. Captain Strelnikov shot down one Bf 109 that came down three to four kilometres south of Elvines. Senior Lieutenant Batrakov shot down one Bf 109 that crashed near Fischevann.

Following the fighter-bombers, the targets in Kirkenes were attacked by Bostons of the 5th MTAD. They dropped bombs on the port and the ore processing plant. It is known from German documents that a stack of ammunition prepared for evacuation exploded on the pier. Two Bostons were shot down by anti-aircraft fire over the target, their crews were killed.

Attack aircraft of the 46th GKAP struck German ships and vessels in the Lang Fjord.

The German records on losses of ships and aircraft for that day are quite incomplete. Some documents indicate the loss of the artillery barge AF-57 during this attack. The artillery barge AF-25 was damaged, with two men killed and eight wounded (including the barge's commander). The high-speed landing barge F-201 suffered steering failure and leaks from small holes. However, both damaged barges were repaired by the Germans. Other German ships and vessels may have been damaged as well. It is known for certain that no loading operations were carried out in the port at all on that day due to the raids.

3 Historical note: the motor minesweeper R-151 was built in Burg Lezum at the Burmester factory. Put into service on 18 July 1940. Was part of 7th Motor Minesweeper Flotilla. Standard displacement – 110 tonnes. Total displacement – 126 tonnes. Length – 35m. Width – 5.5m. Depth – 1.5m. Maximum speed – 23.5 knots. Armament: one 37mm gun and several 20mm anti-aircraft guns.

Whilst fulfilling the task of covering the attacking aircraft, an Airacobra of 27th IAP was shot down, its pilot, Junior Lieutenant N.I. Ryabov, was killed.

Luftwaffe fighters from *Stab* III./JG 5 and *Stab* IV./JG 5, the 10., 12. and 15. *Staffeln* of the JG 5 took part in repulsing the attack on Kirkenes. Most of the Luftwaffe fighters attacked the Soviet aircraft as they retreated from their targets in the Luostari area. The Luftwaffe pilots claimed to have shot down 21 Soviet aircraft. According to the records, the Germans lost three fighters that day (two were lost, one crashed during a forced landing). However, one of the fighters was definitely lost in a battle with a Yak-9 near Salmijärvi, so the losses over Kirkenes could have been up to two enemy fighters. However, the details of these losses are not known.

Based on the results of the air combats in the Kirkenes area, the Northern Fleet Air Force Headquarters credited 10 downed Luftwaffe aircraft to the pilots and air gunners. Captains V.P. Strelnikov and P.I. Sakharov, Senior Lieutenant A.I. Batrakov, Lieutenant A.S. Pavlov of the 78th IAP, Lieutenants N.I. Dyogtev and P.M. Demikov and Junior Lieutenant V.M. Kotenko of the 27th IAP were credited one Bf 109 each. One FW 190 each was credited to Captain A.N. Sizov of the 27th IAP, Lieutenant G.A. Dmitrik of the 20th IAP, and Junior Sergeant P.V. Mikhailov – an air gunner of the 46th ShAP.

The losses of the Northern Fleet Air Force during the raid on Kirkenes included one Airacobra and two Bostons with the bombers shot down by anti-aircraft fire.

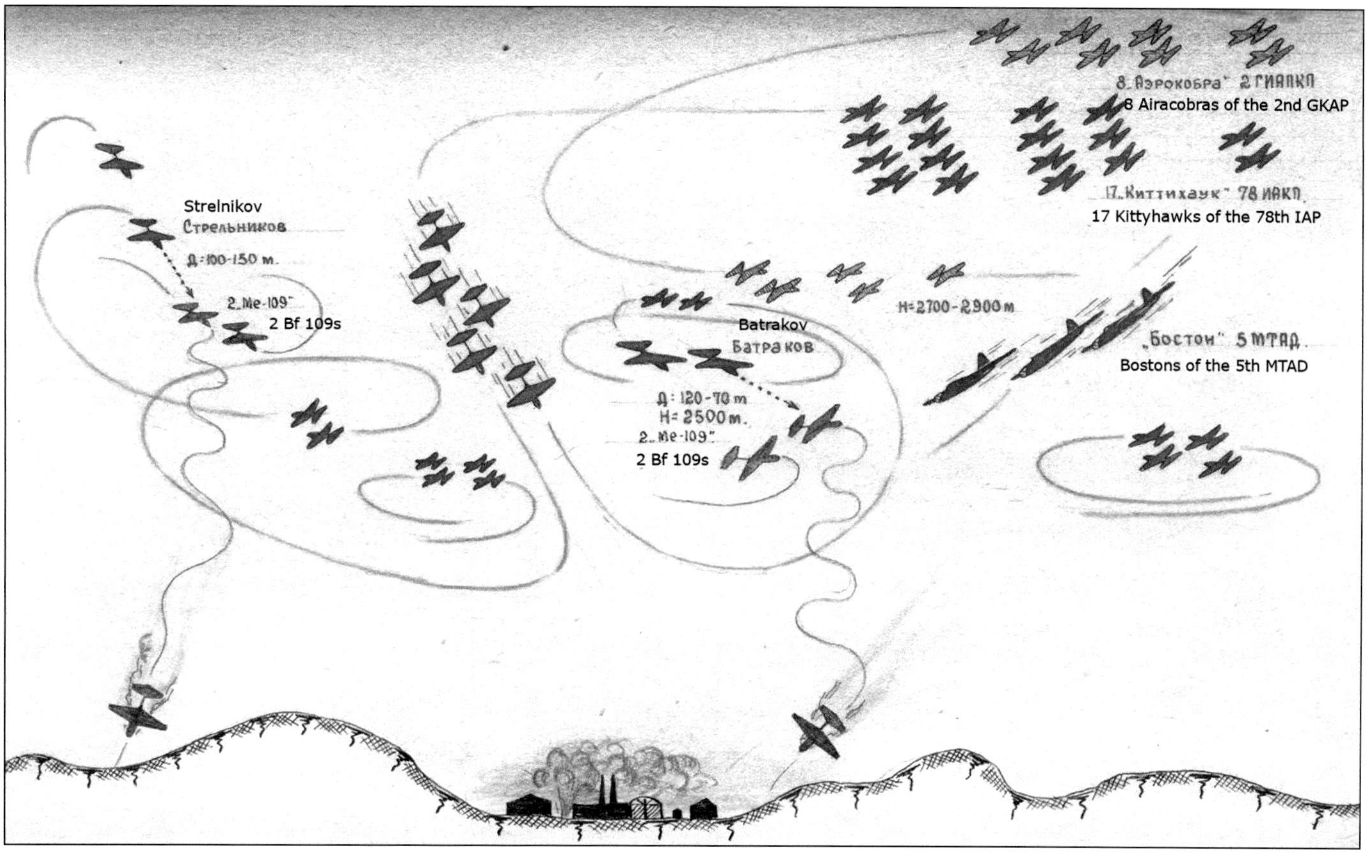

Plan of air combat of the 6th IAD aircraft over Kirkenes on 21 October 1944.

Pilots of the Northern Fleet Air Force observe their comrades returning from a combat mission.

КИРКЕНЕС. 21.10.44 года.

Фотодонесение:

Б/удар по городу.
78 АП. Л-к Кириллов.
АФА-3С. Н=4000 м.
12.41 21.10.44 г.
Мс = 80 м. в 1 см.
С-т "Киттихаук".

Результаты дешифрирования:

1. Одно горящее жилое здание.
2. Три горящих складских помещения
3. Дымовые шашки.

Photo reconnaissance report of the results of the air strike on Kirkenes by Kittyhawks of the 78th IAP on 21 October 1944.
Photo reconnaissance reporting
Bomb strike on the town; 78th IAP, Lieutenant Kirillov; AFA-3S camera; Altitude 4,000m; 12:41, 21 October 1944; Scale – 80 metres in one centimetre; Kittyhawk aircraft.
Results of the photo reconnaissance interpretation
1. One apartment house on fire.
2. Three warehouses on fore.
3. Smoke flares.

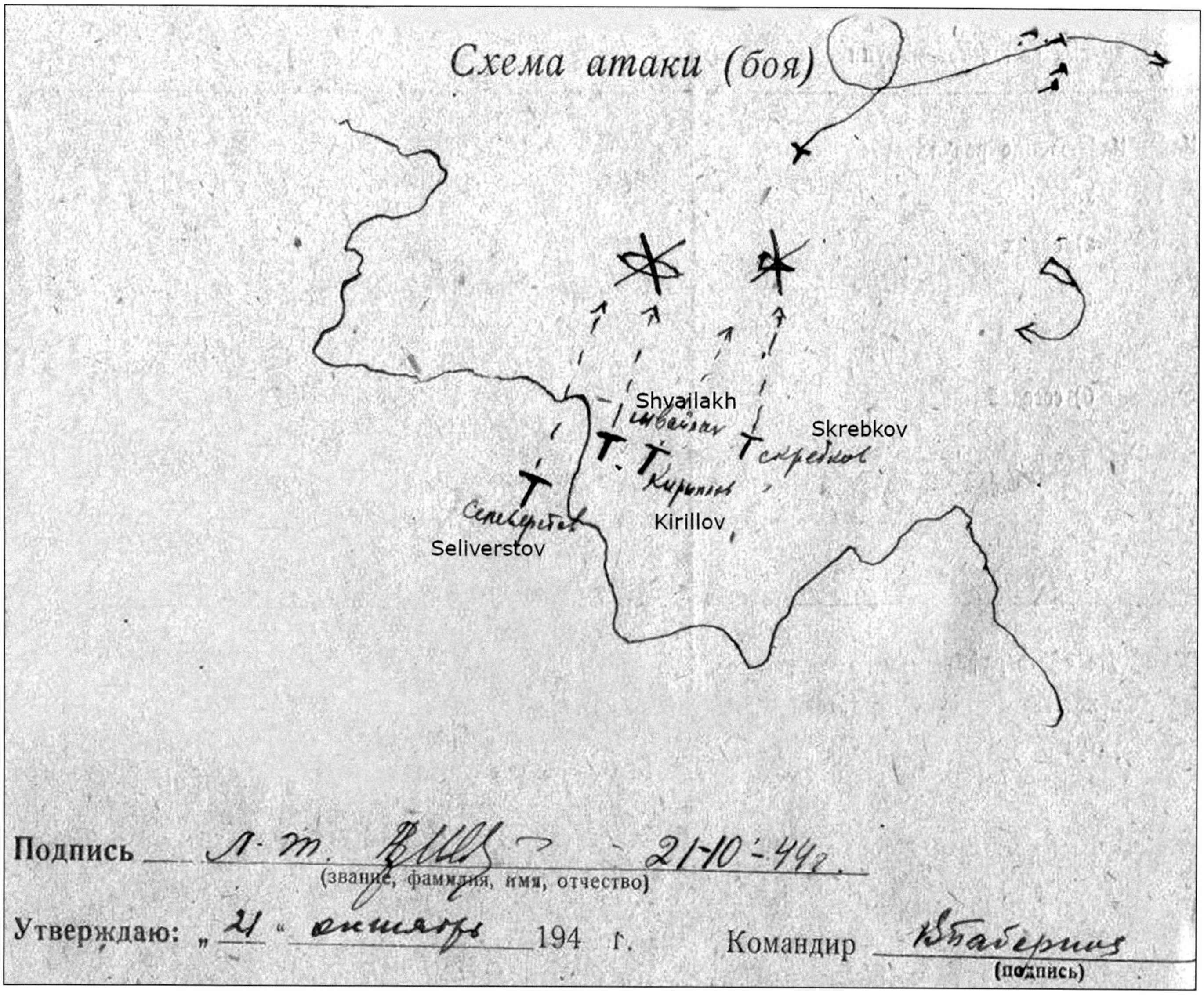

Plan of attack on German ships from the report of the 78th IAP Kittyhawks' leader, Senior Lieutenant A.Ya. Shvailakh, on 21 October 1944.

22 October

On this day the Kittyhawk fighter-bombers achieved a new success. Once again, it was the group of aircraft led by Senior Lieutenant A.Ya. Shvailakh. From the report of Senior Lieutenant A.Ya. Shvailakh:

> Take-off at 10:05, following the route Rosta – Zapadnaya Litsa – Pummanki – Komagnes – Syulte Fjord – Komagnes Cape – Rosta. Flight altitude from low to 100–500m. The aircraft attacked a cluster of enemy ships in Syulte Fjord at 11:00. The bombing attack was unexpected because it was launched from behind hills with the sun behind us. The enemy opened anti-aircraft fire too late. My bombs fell with an undershoot of five metres at the side of a three-masted ship with a displacement of 2,000 tonnes; before bombing, I fired at it with my machine guns. My bombs fell with undershoot due to the following: high masts of the ship, which I could not pass from the required distance of bombing. The bomb dropped by Junior Lieutenant Saranchin fell with 30m undershoot away from the side of the three-masted ship.

Judging by the composition of the convoy, the target of the attack was the sailing ship *Moshulu*. This overly lucky vessel was dragged from Kirkenes in a tug and yet, despite repeated Soviet aviation attacks, it managed to survive. From the further text of Shvailakh's report: "The bombs dropped by Lieutenant Ivanov hit a speedboat and blew it apart". Lieutenant V.P. Ivanov succeeded in achieving a direct hit of FAB-100s on the motor minesweeper R-202, but the bomb failed to explode. The minesweeper, although had been hit in many places by the machine-gun fire, reached the floating base and was repaired. From the same report: "The bombs dropped by Junior Lieutenant Seliverstov hit the engine room of the minesweeper. The minesweeper was instantly covered in smoke and steam. On moving away from the target, we observed it sinking".

Referring to the report of the mechanical engineer of the 63rd Patrol Boat Flotilla about the damage of the patrol ship V-6308:

> During the air raid the ship received two direct hits from bombs and sustained severe machine-gun fire. The first bomb exploded in the radio room on the port side and caused heavy fire. The second bomb fell on the boat deck, behind the funnel. The boiler and steam line of the main and auxiliary engines were badly damaged by the blast wave and splinters. Due to the damage to the steam boiler, there was a threat of an explosion. The boiler was extinguished. The boiler room and engine room were then inspected and it was found that the damage could not be repaired by the ship's crew and a workshop repair was required. The fires which occurred after the first bomb hit in the radio room, Commander's and the

First Officer's quarters were extinguished with the help of V-6312 and R-63.

The crew of the patrol ship V-6308 lost four sailors dead and six wounded. The ship became disabled and was taken on tow by the submarine hunter UJ-1206. The patrol boat was saved by the Germans and was towed to Bergen, where it was being repaired at least until the end of January 1945. It survived the war and in September 1945 it worked for the German Mine Sweeping Administration (GM/SA).

None of the pilots observed that they had damaged another German ship. From the report of mechanical engineer of the 63rd Patrol Boat Flotilla on the damage of V-6311:

> At 08:55, the ship was attacked by four Il-2s. Cannon and machine-gun fire. Steam lines to main and auxiliary engines were punctured. Due to this, they are out of order. The steam line was repaired by the crew. At 23:30, the engine was again running at six knots.

While the patrol boat V-6311 was repairing the steam line, it was being towed by the submarine hunter UJ-1207. All four Kittyhawks returned safely to Rosta airfield.

24 October

On this day, the Kittyhawks of the 78th IAP fought their last air battles and achieved their last victories over enemy aircraft. Unfortunately, they did not avoid losses.

On the evening of 23 October, a convoy Ki.141.Lf left Kirkenes. This was the seventh and last evacuation convoy. The convoy consisted of gunboat K-3, patrol ships V-6111, V-6703, V-6713, Nki-03, Nki-05, Nki-08, minesweepers M-302, M-322, M-382, motor minesweepers R-56, R-63, R-90, R-238, R-250, R-300, R-302, R-307, R-308, artillery gun barge AF-25, steamship *Adamsturm* (1,923grt), tankers *Kloveren* (428grt) and *Adlergrund* (669grt), tugboats *Giselau*, *Lemwerder* and *Kurefjord*.

A reconnaissance Boston of the 118th RAP spotted the convoy near Makkaur Cape at about 10:00 on 24 October.

At about 11:00, a group of 18 Il-2s of the 46th ShAP under the cover of Yaks of the 20th IAP and eight Kittyhawks of the 78th IAP attacked the German ships in Tana Fjord. The incompleteness of German documents makes it impossible to accurately assess the results of the strike.

On the way back, the Soviet aircraft were attacked by FW 190s of 13./JG 5. From the combat flight log of the 6th IAD: "In the target area the aircraft were engaged in air combat against four FW 190s; Captain Sakharov shot down one FW 190". Based on the results of the air combat Captain P.I. Sakharov was credited with one downed FW 190. The Luftwaffe fighters, in their turn, severely damaged one Kittyhawk. From the report on the loss of the aircraft: "I was accompanying Il-2s during a bombing attack against the enemy ships in Tana Fjord. On the way back, the aircraft was attacked by four FW 190s in the area of Berlevåg; as a result, the hydraulic system of flaps and the engine were damaged. The aircraft nosed over. As a result, the aircraft was wrecked". The

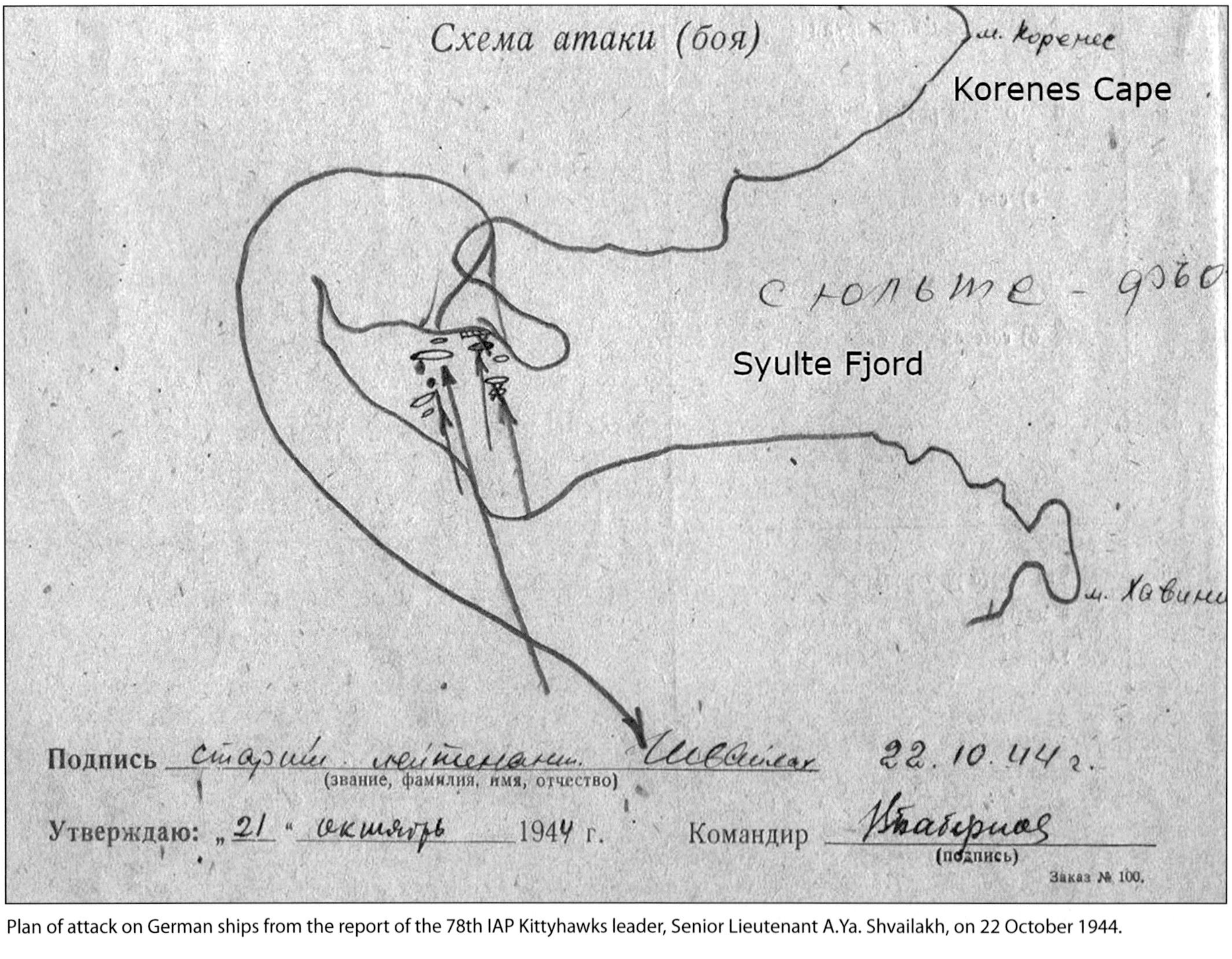

Plan of attack on German ships from the report of the 78th IAP Kittyhawks leader, Senior Lieutenant A.Ya. Shvailakh, on 22 October 1944.

pilot, Junior Lieutenant A.E. Yevdokimov, was not injured in the battle, but suffered from the command, which reprimanded him for unsuccessful landing.

However, this air combat was not the last one that day. Two hours later, the convoy was attacked by groups of fighter-bombers and torpedo bombers. According to the plan of the Northern Fleet Air Force Headquarters, the convoy was to be attacked by Kittyhawk fighter-bombers in order to suppress the anti-aircraft artillery of the convoy, followed by the torpedo bombers. In fact, the torpedo bombers were the first to attack.

The convoy was attacked by 10 Boston torpedo bombers of the 5th MTAD: three high-altitude torpedo bombers of the 36th MTAP (leader – Captain P.P. Gusev), three low-altitude torpedo bombers of the 9th MTAP (leader – Guards Lieutenant A.G. Lukashev), and four of the 36th MTAP (leader – Captain V.P. Novitskiy).

Lieutenant M.I. Masyukov, pilot of reconnaissance aircraft of the 118th RAP, wrote in his report about the subsequent events: "At 12:45, from an altitude of 2,500m, I observed an attack of low-altitude torpedo bombers; the attack resulted in the sinking of a patrol ship". German documents confirm the loss of the patrol ship V-6111. The ship of 1,000 tonnes displacement was hit in the bow by a torpedo and was finished off by the Germans themselves. A torpedo hit killed nine German sailors.

Luftwaffe fighters did not resist the attack of the torpedo bombers, but three torpedo bombers of the 9th GMTAP and one of the 36th MTAP were shot down by anti-aircraft fire.

After the torpedo bombers' strike, 12 Kittyhawk fighter-bombers of the 78th IAP (leader – Senior Lieutenant A.I. Batrakov) attacked the convoy. They split into two groups, with four aircraft dropping bombs on the lead guard ships and the rest on the tail guard ships. All Kittyhawks dropped bombs from a dive, from an altitude of 2,500m. Some documents indicate that four Kittyhawks attacked by the skip-bombing method, but reports from the pilots refute this. From the report of Senior Lieutenant A.I. Batrakov, leader of the group of Kittyhawks: "Four Kittyhawks attacked the tail guard ships. Bombs were dropped on a patrol boat. When approaching the convoy, I observed the explosion of the transport and sinking of the latter [due to torpedo attacks – Author's note]".

One Kittyhawk was shot down by anti-aircraft fire from German ships. From the accident report on the loss of aircraft: "At 12:46, the aircraft was fired at by anti-aircraft artillery at the target area, the engine was damaged by shell splinters. The pilot was so distracted by the attack, that he flew at a low-level, and as a result was hit by anti-aircraft machine-gun fire. The propeller pitch controller was damaged. The propeller was at high pitch. The pilot managed to return to friendly territory. Near Pummanki he had to ditch the aircraft. The aircraft sank, the pilot was rescued". For the pilot of the Kittyhawk, Junior Lieutenant M.V. Tishchayev, it was his first flight, and almost became his last.

Meanwhile, Senior Lieutenant A.I. Batrakov spotted a Luftwaffe reconnaissance Ju 88D-1/Tr of the 1.*(F)/Aufklärungsgruppe* 124 over the convoy. From the report of Senior Lieutenant A.I. Batrakov:

> In the area of Makkaur Cape, at 900–800m above clouds, I met a Ju 88. I attacked the latter. The Ju 88 was flying southward. I made five attacks after which the port engine and the wing caught fire; the Ju 88 turned to Banak. I continued the pursuit and made another six to eight attacks on the starboard engine, the latter also caught fire. When the Ju 88 banked to the right, I received four bullet hits to the engine and in the propeller spinner from the air gunner. After that I made three more attacks from the left from above. The Ju 88 went down in the area of mountain 406 Jakobselevvedden. The Airacobras were attacking from behind from above, from a distance of 300–200m. The Ju 88 was pursued by one Airacobra which attacked one or two times at the beginning of the pursuit and two times from behind from above and on the right at the end.

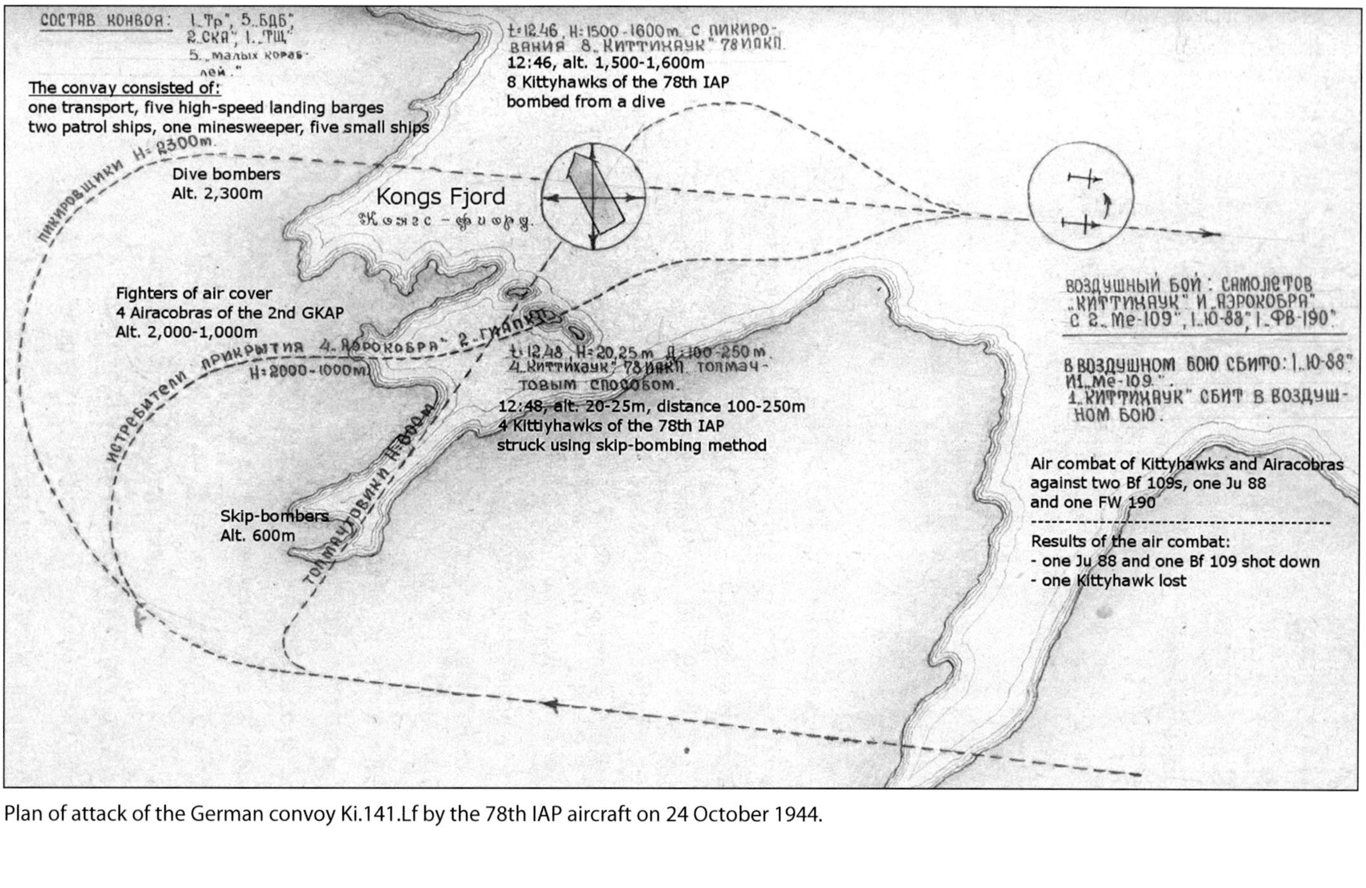

Plan of attack of the German convoy Ki.141.Lf by the 78th IAP aircraft on 24 October 1944.

Lieutenant N.I. Zapalenov of the 2nd GKAP helped to finish off the Ju 88. The Northern Fleet Air Force Headquarters credited the downed Junkers to him.

When returning to base after attacking the convoy, the Kittyhawks were attacked by FW 190s from 13./JG 5. Luftwaffe fighters shot down one Kittyhawk in a surprise attack. From the accident report on the loss of the aircraft: '"At 12:50pm, in the vicinity of Makkaur Cape, while returning home, the aircraft was suddenly attacked from the clouds, from behind and above, and was shot down by an enemy Bf 109. After the first attack it caught fire and went down south of Sylte Fjord". The pilot of downed Kittyhawk, Junior Lieutenant A.A. Seliverstov, died. The Germans had no time to celebrate their victory. From the report of Junior Lieutenant I.N. Guguev:

> On returning, we were engaged in air combat against one FW 190 and one Bf 109 at a low altitude of 100–200m. As a result, I shot down one Bf 109 which, after three long bursts, caught fire and fell in the Ryugden mountain area, Height 497, five to seven kilometres south-west. The Bf 109 was shot down on a combat turn, firing at it at 1/2–3/4 target aspect ratio, the enemy aircraft was following the leading FW 190.

Actually, it was a FW 190F-8, W.Nr. 580964, which was piloted by *Feldwebel* Gustav Scharwächter. The Luftwaffe pilot was unable to escape the doomed aircraft.

After the air combat, the Kittyhawks attacked the retreating German troops. From the report of Junior Lieutenant I.N. Guguev: "In the Skalvanes area I fired machine-guns at fuel trucks in five approaches. As a result of the fire, four trucks with fuel were burnt, a staff bus was destroyed". The Germans confirmed the attacks on the marching columns at Reichstrasse 50 and near Vadsø, which resulted in insignificant casualties.

Meanwhile, convoy Ki.141.Lf continued to retreat westward. Around 21:30, the patrol ship Nki-05, which was following as part of the convoy guard ships, got blown up on a mine after which the crew was evacuated and the ship was finished off by the Germans. It became the second and last ship to be lost by the last German evacuation convoy.

25 October

On this day, the fighter-bombers of the 78th IAP managed to achieve new successes, but again there were aircraft losses.

A group of five fighter-bombers and one photo reconnaissance Kittyhawks (leader – Captain V.P. Strelnikov) flew on a 'free hunting' mission along the Norwegian coast. The aircraft took off from the Rosta airfield at 10:12. They spotted German ships in the Bos Fjord area. From the report of Captain V.P. Strelnikov:

> At 11:05, in Bos Fjord we attacked a transport of 2,000–2,500 tonnes displacement, a barge of 600–800 tonnes, and a patrol boat of 70–100 tonnes by skip-bombing method from an altitude of 20–25m. Range 100–150m. I observed the hit of my FAB-100s in the transport of 2,000–2,500 tonnes in the centre of the ship and one FAB-100 of Junior Lieutenant Novoseltsev.

Several German transports and warships were present in the area of the attack. One of the transports, the *Margareta* (369grt), ran aground on 23 October, and, according to some reports, the Germans were still trying to save it, while according to other sources they blew it up. It is very likely that it was the target of the attack carried out by Captain V.P. Strelnikov and Junior Lieutenant L.I. Novoseltsev. Anti-aircraft fire from German ships was fatal for the Kittyhawk piloted by Junior Lieutenant L.I. Novoseltsev. From the accident report on the loss of the aircraft: "In the course of the 'free hunting' mission in Varanger Fjord, while bombing the enemy ships in Bos Fjord, the aircraft was fired at by anti-aircraft artillery from the destroyer, the aircraft was damaged and made a force-landing in Kola Bay due to engine failures". Everything ended well for the pilot – he was rescued by boats.

While Captain V.P. Strelnikov and Junior Lieutenant L.I. Novoseltsev were attacking the transport of 2,000 tonnes displacement, Lieutenant D.P. Dzyuba found another target. His report: "My two FAB-100s directly hit the self-propelled barge stationed at the pier. The barge exploded". However, the German documents can't confirm the damage caused by the pilot.

The German anti-aircraft gunners from the ships managed to damage the aircraft of Lieutenant D.P. Dzyuba. From the accident report on the damage of the aircraft: "During a bombing attack on the ships in Bos Fjord, the aircraft sustained heavy fire from the anti-aircraft artillery of the destroyer. As a result, the port wing and the port landing gear leg were damaged, and the aircraft requires repair". The aircraft eventually went to the repair shops while the pilot returned unharmed.

Two Junior Lieutenants, I.N. Guguev and I.M. Baev, were the most successful. From the report of Junior Lieutenant I.N. Guguev: "I and my wingman attacked the cluster of patrol ships and motorboats moored at the pier. I observed my bombs hitting a patrol boat which quickly submerged". The accuracy of the German anti-aircraft gunners should be acknowledged – on the return to Rosta airfield it was found out that the aircraft of Junior Lieutenant I.N. Guguev had holes in the fuselage, a control cable was broken, and the radio receiver was smashed. However, all the damages were repaired in a matter of a day by the regiment's technicians.

Junior Lieutenant I.M. Baev reported further: "Junior Lieutenant Guguev struck a patrol boat with a direct bomb hit. My bombs directly hit the speedboat". German documents confirm that the motor minesweepers R-90 and R-250 were hit by one bomb each. The bomb hit the bow of the motor minesweeper R-250 and severely damaged the ship.[4] As a result, the Germans were forced to sink the minesweeper. Another motor minesweeper, R-90, was seriously damaged by the bomb explosion, one crew member was killed and one wounded. However, this time the Germans were able to save the ship.

Junior Lieutenant I.V. Braiko was piloting a photo reconnaissance aircraft and recorded the results of the strike.

26 October

The first success of the day was achieved by a group of four fighter-bombers and one photo reconnaissance Kittyhawks of the 78th IAP (leader – Lieutenant A.Y. Shvailakh). Having flown out on a 'free hunting' mission along the coast of northern Norway, they spotted a group of German ships in the area of Syulte Fjord.

At 9:55, the Kittyhawks attacked the ships using the skip-bombing method and achieved one bomb hit on the motor minesweeper R-302. After dropping their bombs, the aircraft made two attack

4 Historical note: Motor minesweeper R-250 was built in Swinemünde at the Bürmester plant, put into service on 24 July 1944 as part of the 5th Motor Minesweeper Flotilla. Standard displacement – 140 tonnes. Total displacement – 148 tonnes. Length – 39m. Width – 5.7m. Depth – 1.6m. The maximum speed was 22.5 knots. Armament – one 37mm cannon and several 20mm anti-aircraft guns.

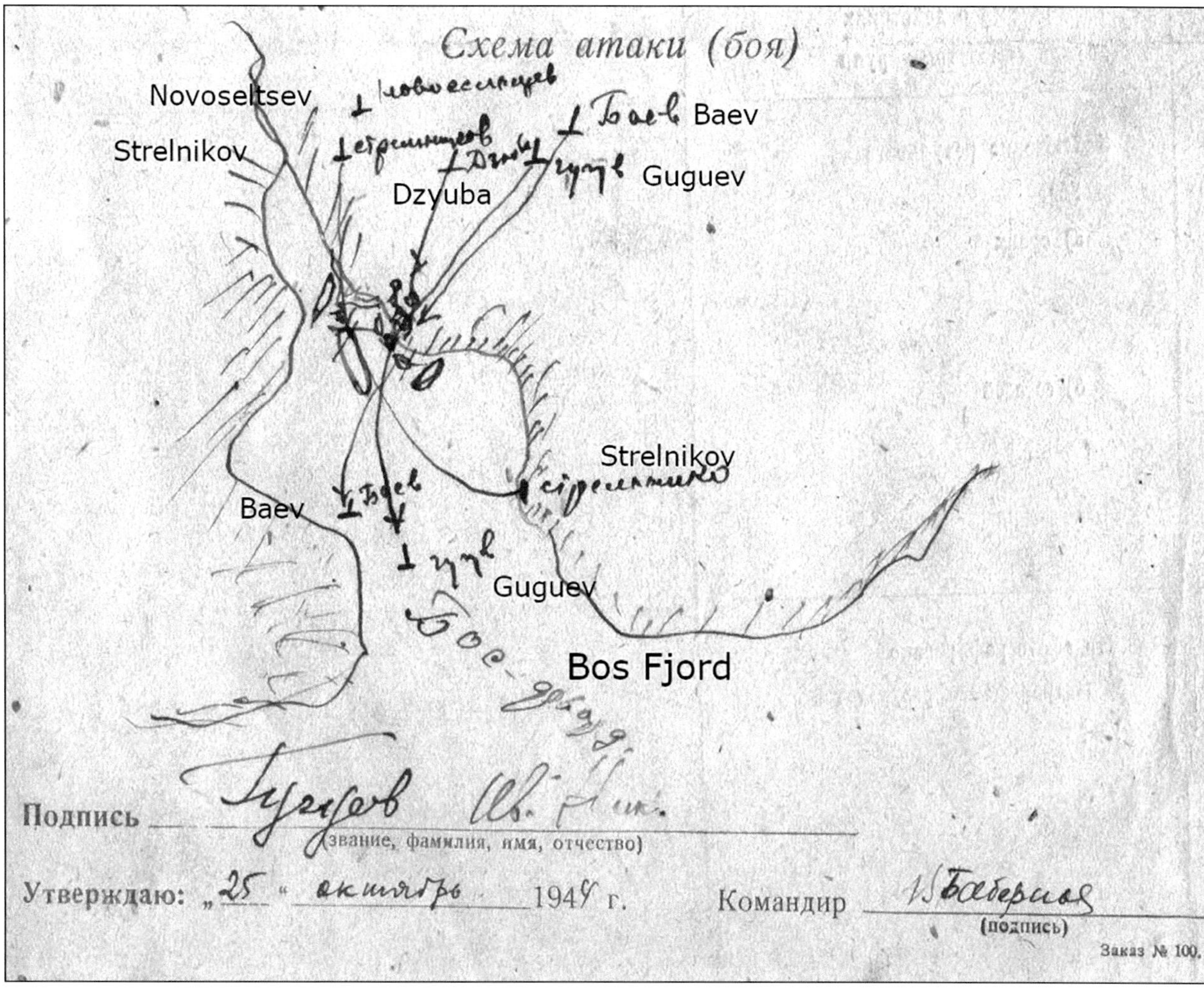

Plan of attack of German ships from the report of the 78th IAP Kittyhawk pilot, Junior Lieutenant I.N. Guguev, on 25 October 1944.

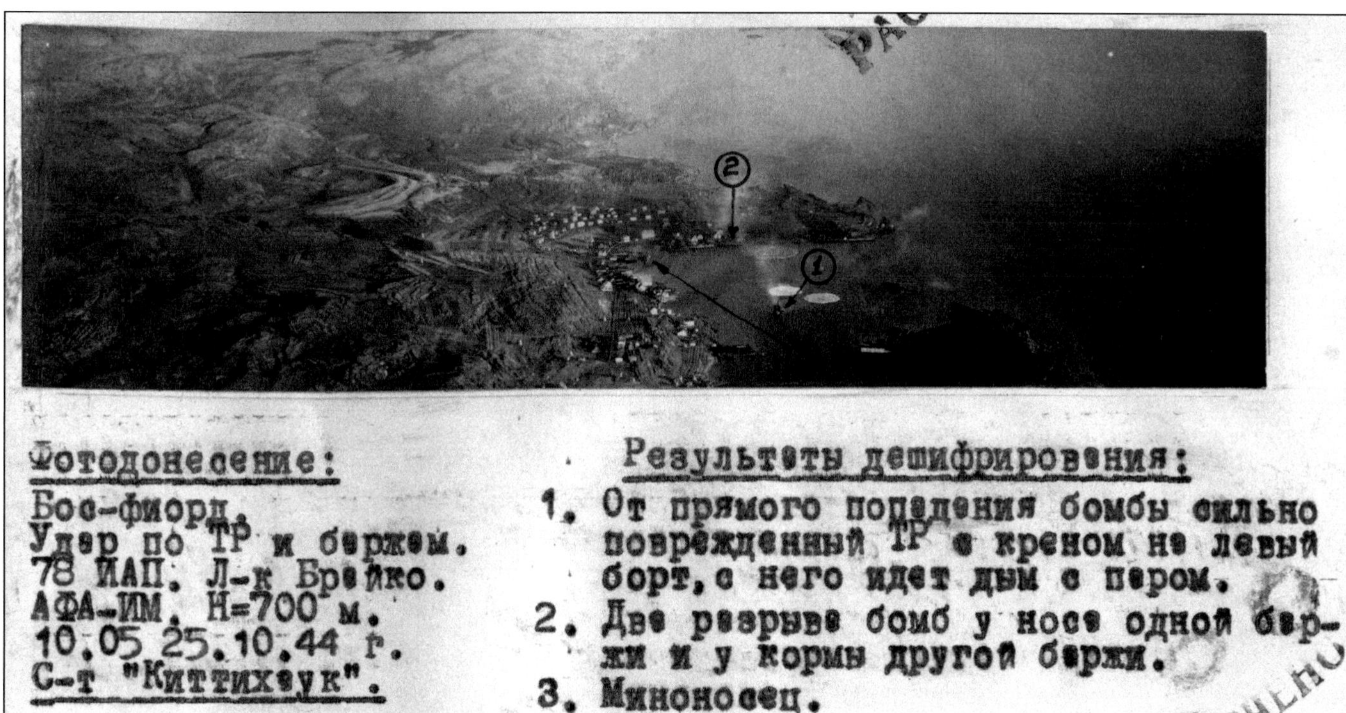

Фотодонесение:
Бос-фиорд.
Удар по ТР и баржам.
78 ИАП. Л-к Брайко.
АФА-ИМ. Н=700 м.
10.05 25.10.44 г.
С-т "Киттихаук".

Результаты дешифрирования:
1. От прямого попадения бомбы сильно поврежденный ТР с креном на левый борт, с него идет дым с паром.
2. Два разрыва бомб у носа одной баржи и у кормы другой баржи.
3. Миноносец.

Photo reconnaissance report of the results of the air strike by Kittyhawks of the 78th IAP on 25 October 1944.
Photo reconnaissance reporting
Bos Fjord; Bomb strike on transports and barges; 78th IAP, pilot Braiko; AFA-IM camera; Altitude 700m; 10:05, 25 October 1944; Kittyhawk aircraft
Results of the photo reconnaissance interpretation
1. After direct hit of the bomb, significantly damaged transport listing to port, emitting smoke and steam.
2. Two bomb explosions – near bow of one barge and near stern of the other.
3. Destroyer.

Pilots and technician near a Kittyhawk.

approaches on the German ships. The strike resulted in damage to the minesweeper. A bomb explosion disabled the port engine of the ship, wounding three crewmen.

Eight Kittyhawk fighter-bombers of the 78th IAP (leader – Captain P.I. Sakharov) which appeared over Tana Fjord at 11:44 did not achieve much greater success. According to German documents, their attack resulted in the sinking of a motorboat and damage to a pier. However, heavy anti-aircraft fire from German ships resulted in the loss of one Kittyhawk. From the report on the loss of the aircraft: "While diving on the target, the aircraft was hit by anti-aircraft fire directly to the engine and crashed on the western shore of Lake Sunewann". The pilot of the Kittyhawk, Junior Lieutenant L.I. Pustobaev, died. It was his 34th combat flight. The aircraft and the pilot were the last combat loss of the 78th IAP during the war.

Six Kittyhawk fighter-bombers of the 78th IAP (leader – Captain V.P. Strelnikov) achieved the last success of the day against enemy ships. The group took off at 12:40 from Rosta. The task of the group was to finish off the 2,000-tonne transport stranded aground in Bos Fjord; it was probably the wreck of the *Margareta* transport ship (369grt). From the report of Captain V.P. Strelnikov:

> At 13:30, in Bos Fjord I attacked [by skip-bombing method – Author's note] a transport of 2,000–3,000 tonnes displacement that had been damaged on 25 October. I observed a hit of my two FAB-100s; as a result of the strike the ship caught fire and began to sink. After my hit the transport caught fire. It was inexpedient to expend more bombs on it, because two FAB-100s had been previously dropped on this transport on 25 October.

After the attack, the Kittyhawks continued the search for enemy ships and at 13:45 they attacked a motorboat in the Pers Fjord. From the report of Senior Lieutenant V.G. Mitrofanov: "I attacked a motorboat in the Pers Fjord at 13:45. My bombs fell with undershoot. The bombs of other pilots fell with overshoot".

29 October

On this date the fighter-bombers, together with the attack aircraft of the 46th ShAP, made the last two strikes against the German ships in Troll Fjord.

At 13:05, 12 Il-2s (leader – Senior Lieutenant N.N. Surovov and Lieutenant N.I. Khilinskiy) together with eight Kittyhawk fighter-bombers of the 78th IAP (leader – Captain P.I. Sakharov) attacked the ships in Troll Fjord under the cover of 16 Yak fighters of the 20th IAP. The pilot of one Il-2, Junior Lieutenant L.I. Ryabov, reported damage to the patrol ship.

At 16:00, 10 Il-2s (leader – Senior Lieutenant N.N. Surovov and Lieutenant N. Khilinskiy) together with eight Kittyhawk fighter-bombers of the 78th IAP (leader – Captain P. Sakharov), under the cover of nine Yak fighters of the 20th IAP, repeatedly attacked the German ships in Troll Fjord. The Kittyhawks were the first to attack, dropping bombs from a dive on the German ships. From the report of Lieutenant A.G. Molchanov, a pilot of the Kittyhawk of the 78th IAP: "While performing a bombing attack against enemy ships in the Troll Fjord, I observed a direct hit of the bombs dropped by my wingman Junior Lieutenant Sokov on the submarine hunter boat standing north of the transport. The submarine hunter boat was not observed on the surface of the fjord after the strike. The bombs dropped by Captain Sakharov fell near the stern of the transport ship,

Photo reconnaissance report of the results of the air strike by Kittyhawks of the 78th IAP on 26 October 1944.
Photo reconnaissance reporting
Bos Fjord; 78th IAP, pilot Braiko; AFA-IM camera; Altitude 400m; 13:30, 26 October 1944; Kittyhawk aircraft
Results of the photo reconnaissance interpretation
Repeated strike on the transport which has been damaged on 25 October 1944.
1. After direct hit of the bomb, the transport is sinking.

after which I observed it smoking from the stern. After the attack of the Il-2 group, I observed one patrol boat smoking and explosions of bombs 5–10m away from the transport". Based on the results of the fighter-bomber attack, the Northern Fleet Air Force Headquarters credited the Kittyhawk pilots with one sunken patrol boat.

The Kittyhawks were followed by the Il-2s of the 46th ShAP. Junior Lieutenant A.N. Ustimenko reported damage to a 2,000-tonne transport and Junior Lieutenant M.A. Tikhomirov reported damage to a patrol boat.

According to available German documents there was a lighter, a coastal tanker and a motor-sailing boat in Troll Fjord. All of them sustained damage but were subsequently towed away by the Germans.

Based on the results of Petsamo-Kirkenes offensive operation, the 78th IAP received a well-deserved reward – on 31 October 1944, the Presidium of the USSR Supreme Soviet issued a decree awarding the 78th IAP of the Naval Air Force with the Order of the Red Banner 'For exemplary performance of the command assignments in the battles against the German invaders, for the capture of the city of Petsamo (Pechenga) and the valour and courage displayed therein'.

5
CONCLUSIONS

In the Northern Fleet Air Force, the Kittyhawks well performed as fighter, fighter-bomber and reconnaissance aircraft.

The fighter version performed quite well in 1942, but by the end of 1943–1944, the better performance of the new Bf 109Gs became obvious. Nevertheless, the Kittyhawks were quite successful in covering attack aircraft in close-cover groups.

The fighter-bomber version was the most well-known, but it had its downsides. Despite its impressive list of sunk ships and vessels, the Kittyhawks were able to sink only one transport and one submarine hunter out of all large ships (over 500 tonnes) according to confirmed data drawn from the both sides. In addition, several German ships were severely damaged.

It should be noted that a large number of small German ships were sunk and damaged by the Kittyhawks. The reason for that was that the aircraft could carry only a small bomb load, which usually amounted to a couple of FAB-100s. Even the direct hit of two of these bombs often did not result in critical damage to the ships.

Strikes against ground targets can be called successful, but in Kirkenes, in addition to the Kittyhawks, other aircraft carried out strikes against the city, and the results of strikes against coastal batteries and troops were no higher, if not lower, than those of the 46th ShAP attack aircraft, according to German documents.

The Kittyhawk reconnaissance aircraft showed their best side because of the high range and good flying performance. It should be noted that only two reconnaissance Kittyhawks were lost in combat missions over a period of almost one and a half years.

The pages of this book do not mention the Kittyhawks that were in service in other units in the Northern Fleet Air Force, but those units were mostly not involved in combat. On the whole, the Kittyhawks, with some reservations, successfully coped with the tasks assigned to them and, together with other aircraft of the Northern Fleet Air Force, brought Victory Day closer.

APPENDIX I: KITTYHAWK LOSSES NOT MENTIONED IN THE TEXT

On 31 March 1944 one Kittyhawk was written off in the 78th IAP because it could not be delivered to the unit. This Kittyhawk made a forced landing on 10 February 1944 and, according to the reports of the regiment technicians, could not be repaired.

On 25 April 1944 one Kittyhawk was written off in the 78th IAP for a similar reason. This Kittyhawk made forced landing on 11 February 1944, 1.5km eastward from Mezen.

On 21 May 1944 two Kittyhawks, which were at the Köchte airfield, were written off in the 78th IAP due to impossibility of being repaired. The aircraft were probably damaged by the regiment pilots during the conversion training from Hurricanes to Kittyhawks.

On 17 July 1944 the 78th IAP lost one Kittyhawk when a pilot of the 20th IAP, Lieutenant Manukov, on take-off turned to the left and hit a parked Kittyhawk of the 78th IAP. During the collision both aircraft were burnt out. The pilot received burns and bruises.

On 25 July 1944 one Kittyhawk was written off in the 78th IAP due to the impossibility of it being repaired.

APPENDIX II: PILOTS OF THE NORTHERN FLEET AIR FORCE, WHO FLEW KITTYHAWK AIRCRAFT AND WERE AWARDED THE TITLE OF HERO OF THE SOVIET UNION

Twice Heroes of the Soviet Union:

SAFONOV Boris Feoktistovich (1915–1942) – squadron commander of the 72nd SAP (awarded on 16 September 1941); commander of the 2nd Guards SAP (awarded on 14 June 1942). Killed in action on 30 May 1942.

Heroes of the Soviet Union:

BOKIY Nikolay Andreevich (1918–1995) – flight commander of the 2nd GKAP (24 July 1943);

DIDENKO Nikolay Matveevich (1921–1975) – deputy squadron commander of the 2nd GKAP (5 November 1944);

KLIMOV Pavel Dmitrievich (1920–1992) – flight commander of the 2nd GKAP (24 July 1943);

KOVALENKO Aleksandr Andreevich (1909–1984) – squadron commander of the 2nd GKAP (14 June 1942);

KOLOMIETS Petr Leontievich (1917–1974) – squadron commander of the 2nd GKAP (5 November 1944);

KURZENKOV Sergey Georgievich (1911–1981) – assistant commander of the 78th IAP (24 July 1943);

ORLOV Pavel Ivanovich (1914–1943) – deputy squadron commander of the 2nd GKAP (24 July 1943); Killed in action on 15 March 1943.

POKROVSKIY Vladimir Pavlovich (1918–1998) – flight commander of the 2nd GKAP (24 July 1943);

SAKHAROV Pavel Ivanovich (1919–1985) – squadron commander of the 78th IAP (5 November 1944);

SGIBNEV Petr Georgievich (1920–1943) – squadron commander of the 78th IAP (23 October 1942); Killed on a training flight on 3 May 1943.

STRELNIKOV Vasiliy Polikarpovich (1919–1993) – squadron commander of the 78th IAP (March 6, 1945).

BIBLIOGRAPHY

Printed books:

Groener, E., *Die deutschen Kriegsschiffe 1815-1945* Band 8 Teile 1 & 2 (Bonn: Bernard & Graefe Verlag, 1993).
Mombeek, E., *Eismeerjager. Zur Geschichte des Jagdgeschwaders 5*, Bde 3-4 (Linkebeek: A.S.B.L., La Porte d'Hoves, 2010-2011).

Archives:

Central Archive of the Ministry of Defence of the Russian Federation, Archive of the Navy branch (Gatchina):
Fund 767. Documents of the Northern Fleet Headquarters.
Fund 787. Documents of the Northern Fleet Air Force Headquarters.
Fund 1980. Documents of the 5th MTAD.
Fund 1982. Documents of the 2nd GIAP.
Fund 1983. Documents of the 78th IAP
Fund 1985. Documents of the 255th IAP.
Fund 1986. Documents of the 46th ShAP.
Fund 1987. Documents of the 118th RAP.
Fund 1988. Documents of the 9th GMTAP.
Fund 2325. Documents of the 27th IAP.
Fund 2452. Documents of the 6th IAD.
Fund 2924. Documents of the 20th IAP.
Fund 2982. Documents of the 95th IAP.
Fund 3283. Documents of the 14th SAD.

The following documents from the U.S. National Archives and Records Administration were provided by Igor Borisenko and Miroslav Morozov:
KTB des Kommandierenden Admirals Norwegen/Oberbefehlshabers des Marineoberkommandos Norwegen 01.01-31.10.1944 NARA T-1022, roll 2750
KTB des Kommandierenden Admiral der norwegischen Polarküste 01.01-15.09.1944, NARA T-1022, roll 2774.
KTB des Küstensicherungsverbandes der norwegischen Polarküste 01-06.1944, NARA T-1022, roll 2777.
KTB des Kommandanten der Seeverteidigung Kirkenes 01.01-30.09.1944, NARA T-1022, rolls 2775-76.
KTB der 5. Landungsflottille 01.07-30.09.1944 NARA T-1022, roll 3137
KTB der 5. Minensuchflottille 01.01-31.10.1944, NARA T-1022, rolls 3079-80.
KTB der 9. Minensuchflottille 01.01-31.10.1944, NARA T-1022, roll 3083.
KTB der 22. Minensuchflottille 01.01-30.09.1944, NARA T-1022, roll 3175.
KTB der 5. Räumbootsflottille 01.05-31.10.1944, NARA T-1022, roll 3437
KTB der 7. Räumbootsflottille 01.01-31.10.1944, NARA T-1022, roll 3492
KTB der 59. Vorpostenflottille 19.01-31.10.1944 NARA T-1022, rolls 3740-41
KTB der 61. Vorpostenflottille 01.01-31.10.1944 NARA T-1022, roll 3791
KTB des Kanonenboote K 3 01.01-31.10.1944 NARA T-1022, roll 3164
KTB MRS Bali 01.01-31.10.1944 NARA T-1022, roll 3883
KTB XIX (Geb.) AK NARA T-314, roll 646

Photos:

Photos are courtesy of the above archives, Finnish Wartime Photograph Archive as well as from the personal archives of the author, Igor Borisenko, Aleksander Mardanov, Miroslav Morozov and Gennady Petrov.

ABOUT THE AUTHOR

Andrey Latkin was born in 1976. He completed his secondary education at St. Petersburg Shipbuilding Technical School, subsequently attending St. Petersburg State University of Telecommunications named after Prof. M.A. Bonch-Bruevich. His primary historical interest lies in the combat actions of the Soviet naval aviation during the Great Patriotic War. In his research, he utilises Soviet documents from the Russian archives and compares the data with available German sources. He has written three books on this subject personally and two more in co-authorship. He has also made approximately 40 articles on the history of the Soviet Navy, which have been published in magazines and on the Internet.